NORTHUMBERLAND

Strange but True

R OBERT W OODHOUSE

The
History
Press

First published in 2005 by
Sutton Publishing.

Reprinted in 2008 by
The History Press, The Mill,
Brimscombe Port, Stroud,
Gloucestershire, GL5 2QG
www.thehistorypress.co.uk

Reprinted 2009, 2011

Copyright © Robert Woodhouse, 2011

**British Library Cataloguing in
Publication Data**
A catalogue record for this book is available
from the British Library.

ISBN 978-0-7509-4067-2

Typeset in 11/13 Photina.
Typesetting and origination by
Sutton Publishing Limited.
Printed and bound in England.

Contents

Winter's Gibbet on Elsdon Moor.

Introduction

As the most northerly of English counties, Northumberland not only faced raiders from across the North Sea and from the south, but also suffered frequent clashes with Scottish clans. Enduring images of those earlier, turbulent days are found in Hadrian's Wall as well as medieval strongholds and pele towers, while Berwick's Tudor fortifications are reminders of the town's ever-changing allegiance to the Scottish or English crowns. The wide expanses of Northumberland attracted some of the early Christian Church's foremost missionaries, and in more recent centuries the county has produced an astonishing number of creative and dynamic men and women.

Every area has its own collection of follies, unusual customs and ecclesiastical oddities, but few locations can compare with the dazzling dimensions of Alnwick's Brizlee Tower, Allendale's spectacular tar-burning ceremony or the mysterious hermitage at Warkworth. The outrageous behaviour of the Delaval family and a series of intriguing inland and coastal features contribute to this collection of remarkable people, places and events which have given Northumberland such a rich and diverse heritage.

All photographs in the book are from the Beamish Photographic Archive or the personal collection of the author. Considerable use has been made of materials supplied by Mr and Mrs H. Johnston.

Drake Stone on Harbottle Crag.

1 Extraordinary People

E very area has its own collection of extraordinary characters, but few
locations can match Northumberland's range of outstanding individuals,
from those with creative and artistic talent to others with a passion for
greater social and political equality. Perhaps it is the rugged beauty of moors and
coastline, inspiration drawn from the waters of rivers such as the Tyne, Tweed
and Coquet or even the harsh realities of life in border country that has inspired
this company of celebrated personalities. Whatever the reason, their achieve-
ments are truly momentous.

Thomas Bewick, arguably Britain's greatest wood engraver, was born at
Cherryburn House near Prudhoe, on 12 August 1753 and died in 1828. The
riverside environment at Cherryburn with a profusion of flower, bird and insect
life may well have nurtured Bewick's natural artistic ability. After schooling at
Ovingham vicarage with Revd Christopher Gregson (vicar from 1747 to 1791),
he joined the company of Ralph Bielby, a Newcastle engraver, as a draughtsman.
Later they formed a partnership, but in 1797 the link was broken and Bewick
set up his own business in a shop in the precincts of St Nicholas's Church (the
Cathedral).

Thomas Bewick was an artist of supreme talent. As a child he is said to
have drawn, carved and sketched on any available material from church porch,
pews and gravestone to any space in books and on papers. The result was
numerous delightful vignettes showing spring flowers, the shimmering heat of a
summer's day, falling autumn leaves and the rawness of winter. These were used
to illustrate books such as Thomsons' *Seasons* and Robert Bloomfield's *Farmer's
Boy*, but his most memorable works feature in *Gay's Fables* (1779), *Select Fables*
(1784), *A General History of Quadrupeds* (1790) and two volumes of *British Birds*
(1797 and 1804). Following his death in 1828 Thomas Bewick was buried in
Ovingham churchyard close to the west side of the tower. A monument in the
chancel has the wording: 'Thomas Bewick, whose genius restored the art of
engraving on wood. The most perfect specimens of his skill are shown in the
history of quadrupeds and British birds.'

Haydon Bridge can also claim an artist of considerable merit. John Martin
was born on the outskirts of the town at East Lands End in 1789, and many
local landscapes feature in his paintings. Spectacular thunderstorms often
brought floods along the Tyne Valley during early summer, and these inundations
inspired such paintings as 'The Deluge' and 'Joshua Commanding the Sun to
Stand Still'.

The home of Thomas Bewick, Cherryburn at Mickley.

A woodcut by Thomas Bewick of four boys sitting on gravestones pretending they are horses.

St Mary's Church, Ovingham.
Thomas Bewick is buried in the
adjacent churchyard.

Memorial to Thomas Bewick inside
St Mary's Church, Ovingham.

John Martin's first exhibit at the Royal Academy, 'Sadak', confirmed his reputation and from this event, in 1812, his stature grew considerably. Over the next forty years Martin's paintings were regularly featured at the Academy, many of them portraying dramatic landscapes and historical events. His best-known works were 'Belshazzar's Feast', 'The Fall of Babylon' and 'Destruction of Herculaneum', which was displayed at the Tate Gallery. Late in life John Martin left London, where he had completed most of his paintings, and died on the Isle of Man in 1854. A street on the southern side of Haydon Bridge has been named after him – a fitting memorial to this famous local son.

Lancelot Brown was born in the remote rural setting of Kirkharle in 1716 and went to the village school in Cambo. On leaving school he was employed as a gardener by Sir William Loraine at Kirkharle, but at the age of twenty-three a move southwards to the home of Sir Richard Grenville at Wetton, near Woodstock, brought opportunities for progression in the world of gardening. After only a year he moved to Lord Cobham's estate at Stowe, where he first worked in the kitchen garden, before becoming head gardener not long after.

On 22 November 1744 Lancelot Brown married Bridget Wayet in St Mary's Church at Stowe, and during the next few years they had six children (though one of their four sons died within weeks). A move to Hammersmith in London in the early 1750s saw him open his own business in which gardening work was combined with architecture. A growing reputation based on successful work

The birthplace of John Martin, East Land Ends, Haydon Bridge.

St Wilfred's Church at Kirkharle, birthplace of Lancelot 'Capability' Brown.

Memorial to Capability Brown in St Wilfred's Church, Kirkharle.

for the Earl of Coventry at Croome Court, Worcestershire, and other schemes in Hampshire, Wiltshire, Suffolk, Kent and Essex resulted in the nickname 'Capability'. During 1757 Brown landscaped Lord Weymouth's estate at Longleat with additional trees and shrubs as well as a restyled lake. His status as a landscape gardener was further enhanced with schemes for the Duke of Northumberland at Alnwick and also at Syon House near Brentford, while other northern projects included the grounds of Harewood House, near Harrogate, and Gibside Hall on Gateshead's western fringe.

In 1764 Capability Brown was appointed royal gardener to King George III with an annual salary of £2,000 and accommodation at Wilderness House, Hampton Court, but he continued to carry out private schemes such as the landscaping of estates around Blenheim Place. Working for the Duke of Marlborough, Brown dammed the River Glyme to create two large lakes and a cascade and planted extensive avenues of trees. During 1767 he bought the Manor House at Fenstanton in Huntingdonshire. Until his death on 6 February 1783 he shared his time between the Manor and Hampton Court. His tomb and those of members of his family, including his eldest son, Lancelot, who became a politician, John, an admiral in the Royal Navy, and Thomas, the rector of the Parish of Fenstanton, are to be found in Fenstanton churchyard. From humble beginnings in an isolated Northumberland hamlet to a prime position in royal circles, Capability Brown made his mark in the most creative of ways, on England's eighteenth-century landscape.

Many local people have made major contributions to areas of academic research. A bronze inscription in the Presbyterian Church of St George near Morpeth Bridge celebrates the work of Dr John Horsley. It reads ' . . . for 23 years minister of this church, Master of Arts in the University of Edinburgh, Fellow of the Royal Society, who died at Morpeth, January 12th 1732 aged 46. This tablet was dedicated in 1932 two hundred years after the publication of his book "Britannia Romana" to record his services to learning as explorer and historian of Roman Britain and to preserve his memory in the town where he lived and taught.' During the course of his research John Horsley travelled all over the country on horseback, and in more recent years his contribution to British archaeology has received widespread acknowledgement.

Most areas produced pioneering agriculturalists during the late eighteenth and early nineteenth centuries, and one of Northumberland's leading figures in the farming world was John Grey. Born in 1785 at West Ord, near Berwick-upon-Tweed, he introduced improved methods of cattle breeding and land cultivation during the early nineteenth century. After building Dilston Hall in the mid-1830s he shared ideas with foreign agriculturists who were entertained in his home. In addition to his farming interests John Grey took an active part in campaigns on contemporary issues. From the age of seventeen he actively supported the movement to abolish slavery by gathering petitions in border towns, and then joined Lord Brougham during his anti-slavery tour of Northumberland and

Cumberland. He was a strong advocate of social reform and played a significant role in the campaign for the 1832 Reform Act and the repeal of the Corn Laws. He lent similar support to the campaign for Catholic emancipation. Perhaps it should be no surprise that his fourth daughter, Josephine, grew up to share her father's religious and moral principles and his strong dislike of inequality and injustice. She became a leading figure in movements for social and political reform during the second half of the nineteenth century.

Josephine Grey was born on 13 April 1828 at Millfield Hill. On 2 January 1852 she married George Butler, an examiner of schools in Oxford. Josephine was undoubtedly influenced by academic life in the city. The Butlers later moved from Oxford when George was appointed vice-principal of Cheltenham College in 1857, and then to Liverpool, where he became principal of the city's college in January 1866. Following the death of her six-year-old daughter Eva, Josephine became involved in charity work, and made efforts to improve women's conditions in the local workhouse. She also played a leading role in developing women's educational prospects as president of the then recently established North of England Council for Promoting Higher Education of Women from 1867 to 1873. During the 1860s the Contagious Diseases Prevention Act was passed in an attempt to reduce venereal disease in the armed forces. However, it aroused considerable opposition as the law only applied to women. The Act gave the police the power to arrest

The grave of Josephine Butler close to the west tower of St Gregory's Church at Kirknewton.

women. In 1869 Josephine Butler formed the Ladies National Association for Repeal. Her relentless campaigning took in continental countries where she won support from personalities such as Guiseppe Mazzini in Italy and Victor Hugo in France. In Britain national figures including Florence Nightingale, Harriet Martineau and Lydia Becker gave their backing to the movement. After some sixteen years the opposition to this legislation was successful. Campaigners had resolutely maintained, through demonstrations and petitions, that the laws were grossly unfair to women and in 1886 they were repealed.

Following her husband's death in 1890, Josephine Butler lived near the home of her eldest son at Wooler where she continued to write pamphlets and books on aspects of social reform and prominent reformers up to her death on 30 December 1906. This redoubtable champion for social reform is buried close to the west tower of St Gregory's Church at Kirknewton.

Emily Wilding Davison is probably Britain's best known political campaigner. Born at Longhorsley on 11 October 1872, she enjoyed a comfortable middle-class upbringing and graduated from London University in 1906 before joining the Women's Social and Political Union later that year. Under the leadership of Emmeline Pankhurst, the WSPU campaigned for female suffrage, and although a faction within the organisation continued to use peaceful forms of demonstration, other suffragettes chose a more aggressive approach. Emily became a leading figure in the militant branch of the movement and was arrested and imprisoned on several occasions. While in prison she went on hunger strike, and in Strangeways Prison, Manchester, she became one of the first suffragettes to be forcibly fed. During another period of imprisonment there she barricaded herself in her cell and the incident was only resolved when the cell was flooded with a hosepipe. As a result of this episode in 1909 Emily spent several weeks in the prison hospital, and in the following year she successfully sued for damages against prison magistrates who had ordered the flooding of the cell.

Two years later she was imprisoned in Holloway Prison and almost died after jumping from the prison gallery to the wire netting guard below. The injuries that she sustained resulted in another long period in hospital, but after her release from prison she resumed her leading role in organising demonstrations, protest marches and meetings for women's suffrage. On a number of occasions Emily was found hiding in the House of Commons where she had concealed herself while waiting to confront members of parliament. She travelled to many parts of the country to encourage violent protests, and Northumberland suffragettes responded by burning down Gosforth Hall on the racecourse.

Emily Davison's final dramatic action took place on Derby Day, 4 June 1913. As the leading horses galloped around Tattenham Corner she eased herself under the rails and flung herself under the hooves of King George V's horse, Anmer. The horse stumbled and fell, dislodging the jockey, but both recovered from their injuries. However, Emily's wounds were more serious and she died in hospital four days later. The incident made international headlines and aroused widespread sympathy for the cause of women's suffrage throughout the country. A procession numbering many thousands, wearing the green, white and purple of the suffragette movement, followed the cortége through London before Emily Davison's coffin was transferred to a train for the journey north. There were similar crowds at Morpeth when she was finally laid to rest in the town's church-yard. Her gravestone carries the epitaph: 'Greater love hath no man than this, that he lay down his life for friends. Emily Wilding Davison, born October 11th 1872. Died June 8th 1913. "DEEDS NOT WORDS".'

Little more than a year later Britain and other world powers were plunged into the horrors of the First World War and the part played by women on the Home Front was a major factor in the extension of the franchise to women over thirty years of age in 1918.

Tyneside's development as a major industrial and commercial centre during the first half of the nineteenth century produced many outstanding architects, designers and engineers. Newcastle's population had grown steadily from around 20,000 in 1750 to 35,000 in 1821, but this was followed by a rapid increase to 88,000 in 1851 and there was a pressing need to redevelop the centre of the city. The catalyst for the new project was Richard Grainger (1797–1861) who began his working life as a jobbing builder in partnership with his brother. The early years saw construction of housing in Higham Place (1819) and Blackett Street (1824) as well as the completion of Eldon Square (1824–6) and the Royal Arcade (1831–2).

Grainger's greatest strengths, however, were his capacity to gather huge amounts of development money and a clarity of thought that enabled him to triumph over the complications posed by private ownership and vested interests. He harnessed the talents of architects such as Thomas Oliver (1791–1857) and more notably John Dobson (1787–1865) to develop the area that included Grainger Street, Grey Street and Clayton Street during the late 1830s. The completed project gives strength to Newcastle's claim to be the only large city in England with a planned centre. John Dobson's designs covered a whole range of structures from churches and halls to monuments and bridges, but his most impressive public work must be Newcastle Central station. Opened on 29 August 1850 by Queen Victoria, the innovative structure of curved, wrought-iron ribs, iron columns and glass won a gold medal at the Paris exhibition in 1858.

The north-east's pioneering role in railway development spawned many outstanding engineers. Perhaps best known of these is George Stephenson (1781–1848), who was born at Wylam, close to the Tyne, and is remembered for his leading role in constructing the first public railway on which steam locomotion was used (between Stockton on Tees and Darlington from 1825). Five years later he completed work on the Liverpool and Manchester line, the first railway to carry passengers and the first to be completely steam-operated from the outset. George Stephenson's son Robert (1803–59) was engineer in charge of construction works on two imposing bridges that completed the east coast railway link between London and Edinburgh. The High Level Bridge across the Tyne at Newcastle is composed of six main spans, each of 125ft, that carry the rails at a height of 20ft above the river (with a road deck suspended below the arches). It was officially opened by Queen Victoria on 28 September 1849, some eleven months before she performed the opening ceremony of the Royal Border Bridge at Berwick-upon-Tweed. Spreading some 2,160ft across the river, the viaduct has twenty-eight arches which carry the track 120ft above the water. Robert Stephenson completed both projects for the Newcastle and Berwick Railway Company and was assisted by T.E. Harrison, who later became engineer to the North Eastern Railway.

William Hedley (1779–1843) was born at Newburn, a few miles west of Newcastle, and made a major contribution to the development of steam locomotives. After attending school at nearby Wylam he began work at the local colliery, and in 1813 introduced a system of smooth rails to replace the unreliable rack rails and tooth-wheeled locomotives along the line carrying coal to Newcastle. Hedley's contribution to modifying early locomotives has probably been under-estimated. He is best known for Puffing Billy which ran on the line between Wylam and Newburn. He died in 1843 and is buried in St Michael's churchyard at Newburn.

St Bartholomew's Church, Kirwhelpington. Sir Charles Parsons is buried on the north side of the churchyard.

Charles Algernon Parsons was born in London in 1854, but developed his outstanding talents as a scientist and engineer on the banks of the Tyne. After spending time as a student with W.G. Armstrong & Company at Elswick from 1877, he joined the firm of Clarke Chapman as a junior partner in the early weeks of 1884. As head of the newly established electrical department, Parsons developed a steam turbo generator during his first year, but then left to set up his own work at Heaton. During 1893 he focused on methods for adapting the turbine to marine propulsion, and early in the following year he formed the Marine Turbine Company. Considerable effort was directed into developing a turbine-driven vessel, but it was not until 1897 before SY *Turbinia* was demonstrated at the Naval Review. Following this success the Parsons Marine Steam Turbine Company was established to build marine steam turbines at the Turbinia Works, Wallsend.

In 1906 the battleship HMS *Dreadnought* was commissioned (with turbine) and the following year the *Mauretania* and *Lusitania* were fitted out. Turbines were also adapted to drive centrifugal pumps, fans and blowers.

On their arrival in the north-east during 1884 the Parsons family lived at Corbridge, but soon moved to Ryton before returning to the Tyne Valley, to live at Holeyn Hall, near Wylam, in 1894. A succession of honours including a knighthood were awarded to Parsons – a southerner by birth, but a brilliant engineer whose inventive genius was nurtured and then applied to a range of projects from an industrial base on Tyneside.

William George, 1st Baron Armstrong, is representative of the prodigious amount of industrial and engineering talent that existed on Tyneside during the nineteenth century. Born at Pleasant Row, Shieldfield, Newcastle, on 26 November 1810 he showed an early aptitude for mechanics, but was directed into a career as a solicitor. For thirteen years he pursued a career in the law but his passion for scientific matters remained undiminished, and during the late 1830s he experimented with aspects of hydraulics. In 1840 Armstrong turned his attention to the study of electricity. After researching, writing and lecturing on the subject he was elected a Fellow of the Royal Society while still a practising solicitor.

By the mid-1840s he had successfully promoted the Whittle Dene Water Company and converted a crane at Newcastle docks to include a combined hydraulic ram and pulley device. In 1847 W.G. Armstrong & Company was set up at Elswick, where products such as pumps, lathes and winding engines were manufactured and Armstrong's skills as an innovator ensured the business prospered. Following the Crimean War (1854–6) Armstrong became increasingly involved in the manufacture of armaments. The limitations of the British Army's heavy artillery had been exposed during the war and in 1858, after extensive trials, the 18lb breach-loading gun was one of the many Armstrong weapons recognised as the most dependable and accurate on the market. In return for handing over his patents to the government he received a knighthood and was

Cragside, Rothbury, home of William George, 1st Baron Armstrong.

given responsibilities in the War Department. Between 1859 and 1863 the Elswick Ordnance Works had a monopoly for supplying heavy artillery to British forces, but contracts were ended after a poor showing in Chinese wars. Armstrong resigned from his government posts, amalgamated his ordnance and engineering firms and began to tender for overseas buyers. Although his firm expanded into building warships and then steel-making in general, William Armstrong increasingly withdrew from the industrial setting and concentrated on developing the Cragside estate. His technological skills were devoted to creating an amazing hydraulic system that powered machinery and provided light in buildings throughout the estate.

In 1887 he was created 1st Baron Armstrong of Cragside, and late in life he gave large amounts of money to institutions such as Newcastle's Royal Victoria Infirmary and the Hancock Museum of Natural History. He also gave land that later became Armstrong Park to Newcastle Corporation and endowed the College of Physical Science, which became Armstrong College within Newcastle University. Lord Armstrong died at Cragside, Rothbury, on 27 December 1900 after a lifetime that spanned most of the nineteenth century. His contributions to the world of science and engineering were innovative and far-reaching at local, national and international levels, and through his dynamism and inventiveness, Lord Armstrong perhaps best represents the character and spirit displayed by so many men and women in England's northern border country.

2 Ecclesiastical Oddities

With a range of building styles that often make use of local materials and usually included an assortment of monuments or relics linked with benefactors, church buildings provide a fascinating insight into an area's past. Some aspects hold obvious explanations, but other features are much less clear and need closer investigation to unravel an intriguing background.

While most people would agree that Blanchland rates as one of Northumberland's most attractive villages, few probably appreciate that its layout was greatly influenced by the spreading outlines of an abbey. Founded in 1165 by Walter de Belbec, it housed White Canons of the Premonstratensian Order who survived attacks by Scottish raiding parties before closure came on the orders of King Henry VIII in 1539.

The central feature of the abbey was the thirteenth-century church building, which was considerably longer than the present structure. After standing empty for some two hundred years following closure in 1539, it was restored by Lord Crewe's Trustees who created a curious layout built around the choir, north transept and tower of the original church. The garden of the adjacent Lord Crewe Hotel incorporates the abbey's cloister garth and the hotel stands on the site of the abbey guest house. Although its architecture is distinctly Georgian in style, it is possible to trace original features from the monastery around the doorway and adjoining walls. The abbey's fifteenth-century gatehouse dominates the north side of the village square, which may well have been laid out around the outer court. Much of the village was rebuilt during the mid-eighteenth century to accommodate hordes of lead miners involved in operations on nearby moorland slopes, but much of its charm still originates from the original abbey buildings that used to dominate the north-eastern corner of the community.

Dangers posed by marauding Scots during the medieval period prompted a number of interesting developments in church architecture. A series of impressive castles at locations such as Norham, Warkworth, Etal and Bamburgh bear testimony to the turbulent times that lasted for around three hundred years from the end of the thirteenth century. On a smaller scale, bastle houses such as the one at Black Middens (10 miles north west of Bellingham) offered refuge from invading forces and even churches were forced to place the emphasis on defensive measures. Monastic sites on Lindisfarne and the Farne Islands were strengthened with a protective tower, while Hulne Priory at Alnwick had both a tower and a high perimeter wall.

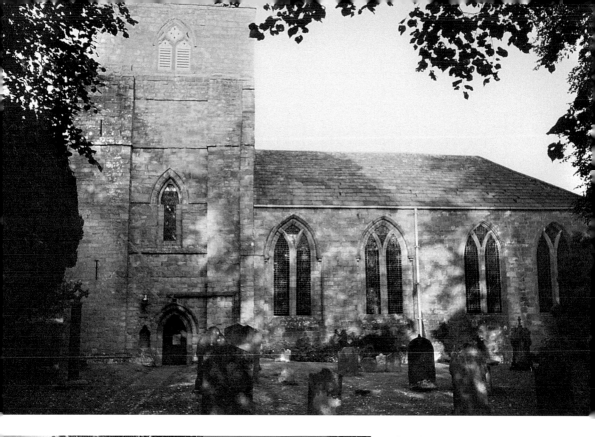

Blanchland Church, fashioned from part of the earlier abbey of Premonstratension canons.

Lord Crewe Hotel, Blanchland, stands on the site of the abbey gues house.

St Cuthbert's Church, Bellingham, with a roof of massive stone slabs.

One of the county's most northerly churches stands beside the Dean Burn at Ancroft. The original building dates from the Norman period, but a prominent pele tower was incorporated into the west end in the early fourteenth century. With thick walls, a tunnel-vaulted ground floor and spiral staircase behind the south doorway, it has much in common with other border tower houses, but looks rather out of place as part of a house of worship.

St Cuthbert's Church of Elsdon has a whole range of unusual features. The fourteenth-century building included side aisles outside lines of arches, but some two centuries later the aisles were demolished and new walls constructed only 4ft from the arches. The new walls had no windows (though they were added in the south wall in 1855) and the refashioned aisles must rank among the narrowest in the whole country. During 1877, when a stone bell turret at the church's west end was being repaired, three horse skulls were found inside a small cavity above the bells. It is believed that they were placed in this remote setting either as protection against lightning or to improve acoustics. Rows of more than a hundred skeletons were unearthed along the north wall of the church during 1810 and 1877. Analysis showed that none of them were of old men or women, and this has led to the conclusion that they were casualties from the Battle of Ottterburn in 1388.

St Gregory's Church, Kirknewton, partly updated by Dobson in the 1860s but retaining a chancel that resembles a pele tower.

The chancel of St Gregory's Church, Kirknewton.

The market town of Bellingham lies on the route taken by Scottish raiders heading down the valley of the North Tyne and, inevitably perhaps, the church of St Cuthbert has been rebuilt several times. The original building dates from about 1200, but the extraordinary roof was put in place some 400 years later. Covering the nave and south transept is a massive roof of stone slabs supported by twenty-two six-sided stone ribs, which was installed after Scottish forces had twice burned down traditional roof timbers. Huge buttresses were added on the north and south sides of the nave during the eighteenth century when the outer walls began to bulge under the weight of the roof.

St Gregory's Church at Kirknewton was partly updated by Dobson in the 1860s, but retains a chancel that has echoes of a pele tower. Small and very low with side walls only 3ft high, it dates from the thirteenth century. A low barrel vault roof and small, narrow windows add to the impression that this tiny area probably served as a place of both worship and refuge.

St Mungo's Church at Simonburn must rate as one of the finest in the county. Originally built during the thirteenth century, it was partly rebuilt in 1762, and further work was carried out on the chancel in 1863. None of the builders seem to have been able to cope with the slope that has left the floor of the church with a rather steep gradient. Interestingly, St Mungo was the illegitimate son of a Pictish princess and went on to become Bishop of Strathclyde.

The tower of All Saints' Church became a landmark on Newcastle's skyline when it was completed in the early 1790s to designs by David Stephenson. It replaced a medieval building on the site and incorporated splendid features, including a detached portico with four Greek Doric columns and sections of balustrading. The overall layout represents one of four oval-shaped churches in the country and Sir John Betjeman described it as 'one of the finest English Georgian churches'. Following deconsecration in 1961, it was adopted for use as office accommodation, but in recent years it has been reconsecrated as the Anglican Old Catholic Church of St Willibrord.

Bedlington is perhaps best known as an important coal mining community, but the discovery of Bronze Age burials indicate a much earlier settlement. St Cuthbert's Church was originally built in the late twelfth century, but most of the present structure is modern. A curious inscription on the west wall of the north aisle, close to the tower, has the words, 'Watson's Wake, 1669', in memory of Cuthbert Watson. On 14 February 1669 he climbed a buttress on the north-east side of the old tower in his sleep. A shout from a passer-by caused him to lose his footing, and in the resulting fall he was fatally injured.

The township of Allendale covers high ground above the river Allen with open moorland on all sides. Most buildings range around a central square with the Victorian St Cuthbert's Church set back from the north-east corner. An unusual feature on its walls is a sundial, which includes an inscription detailing the town's latitude and longitude – a reminder of Allendale's claim to be located at the exact centre of Britain.

All Saints' Church, Newcastle upon Tyne, described by Sir John Betjeman as 'one of the finest English Georgian churches'.

Opposite: All Saints' Church, Newcastle, was completed in the early 1790s to designs by David Stephenson.

Churchyards can often prove to be an invaluable source of information about earlier social and economic trends in town, village or city. The tiny village of Warden is situated close to the confluence of the North and South Tyne with the Church of St Michael overlooking a large churchyard. Among the profusion of memorials, three graves are covered with wrought iron hoops. They mark the final resting places of a past rector, his wife and child and the hoops were put in place at his request in order to foil body snatchers. The churchyard at Morpeth includes a simple single-storey building with only a fireplace to provide warmth for armed watchmen, who kept guard against Resurrectionists (body snatchers). Northumberland was within range of body snatchers who planned to supply medical schools in Edinburgh. The problem reached such a pitch that watch clubs were set up to organise all-night watches in churchyards, especially following fresh burials. At Morpeth the club members built a watch tower to accommodate

The mysterious oblong-shaped gravestone known as the 'Long Pack' in Bellingham churchyard.

two men during two-hour stints, but in recent times the building has taken on an alternative role as a tool shed.

Churchyards with headstones marking burials have existed since the mid-eighth century and carved lettering began to appear in the early seventeenth century. Often this was accompanied by a strange assortment of skulls, skeletons and angels, and one particularly poignant example is to be found at Falstone. It depicts a small girl engaged in a dance of death while holding hands with a skeleton on one side and clutching a posy of flowers in the other hand. Inscriptions on the graves of women usually refer to their godliness and devotion to a husband, but occasionally mention is made of their working life. In the churchyard of St Peter's Church at Bywell a gravestone celebrates a whole lifetime of service in the household of a local family with the succinct sentence 'Sixty years with the Trotters'.

Apart from the fascinating Church of St Cuthbert at Bellingham, the adjacent churchyard holds lots of interest. A simple gravestone from the 1730s is that of Anne Heslope, Midwife – a curiosity from the early days of midwifery and at a time when most women did not have a career or profession. On the north side of the church is a mysterious oblong-shaped gravestone known as the 'Long

Pack'; it is claimed to be linked with a robber who features in Ettrick Shepherd's account of *The Long Pack*. The tale is set in the mid-eighteenth century when a Colonel Ridley retired from a military career in India to Lee Hall on the banks of the nearby North Tyne. During an afternoon in winter the family were away in London when a pedlar called at the homestead and pleaded for overnight lodgings. He was refused admission by servants, but was allowed to leave a strange pack which he claimed was too heavy to carry further. As the maid examined the pack it seemed to move, and other staff were summoned in an attempt to resolve the situation. When a young ploughboy, Edward, arrived on the scheme he fired at the pack with a shotgun. There was a deathly groan from the package and as a pool of blood spread across the floor the group of servants realised that Edward had shot a robber, a member of a gang who intended to raid the hall. A plan was soon prepared with twenty-five armed men on guard around the premises, but nothing happened until the early hours of the next morning when Edward blew a horn that he had found on the body. From the darkness another horn was sounded in reply and galloping hooves were heard approaching the hall. As the horsemen reached the courtyard they were met with a volley of gunfire, and before they withdrew a number of robbers lay dying and injured. Members of the household were afraid to leave the safety of the hall, but when daylight arrived all the bodies had disappeared from sight. It is said that members of several local families were never seen again, and according to the legend the man in the sack remained unidentified and was buried in an anonymous grave.

Coastal locations such as Lindisfarne and the Farne Islands have a place in early Christian history through their links with holy men such as St Aidan and St Cuthbert from the seventh century. Their monastic cells

The entrance to Warkworth hermitage.

The vaulted stonework in the roof of Warkworth hermitage.

The windows of Warkworth hermitage.

could hardly have been in a more remote setting, but during the medieval period a series of priests were based at a fascinating riverside site near Warkworth Castle.

In addition to the chapels and a collegiate church within the castle's walls, the spiritual needs of the household were met by a hermitage that was set in a cliff face overlooking the River Coquet about half a mile away. There are no records of early hermits or dates of their occupancy, but it seems probable that from the outset they were sponsored by the lords of Warkworth. It is clear that the layout of the rooms was altered during the later medieval period when the hermit's duties took on a more earthly dimension. During the late fifteenth century the resident recluse received an annual salary of 66s 8d, but by the 1530s George Lancastre, who served as both hermit and agent to the 6th earl was paid £13 6s 8d. His income was supplemented by grazing land for twelve cattle, a bull and two horses as well as twelve annual loads of firewood and a supply of fish each Sunday.

This curious collection of cliff face caverns is now in the care of English Heritage, with access (during summer months) by ferry from the south bank.

A statue of Paulinus at Holystone.

The pool and stone cross at Holystone.

The upper level includes a little porch with seats on either side and doorway with a folded carving of the crucifixion, the chapel measuring 20½ft by 7½ft, complete with ribbed roof, altar and niche containing weatherworn carvings of the Nativity and the sacristy where sacred vessels were stored in two cupboards on the north wall. Living quarters were located at ground level and date from the fifteenth and early sixteenth centuries. Some of the rooms have been destroyed, but it is still possible to trace the oven among the outlines of the kitchen and a large window in the hall which overlooks the adjacent river. The fireplace displays markers showing the height of devastating floods in 1831 and 1900.

St Paulinus is said to have baptised some 3,000 converts at Holystone (5 miles west of Rothbury) in AD 627, and soon afterwards a small community of Augustinian nuns built a priory close to sacred spring, which is still called Lady's Well. It is believed that the nuns were responsible for converting the well to a rectangular pool during the medieval period. All traces of the priory have now disappeared, but the large basin of clear water still lies in a serene setting amid beech trees. In 1780 the pool was given an edging of stonework and at the centre a tall stone cross was installed with an inscription stating that 'In this place Paulinus the bishop baptised 3,000 Northumbrians. Easter 627'. At one end of the pool there is a weathered statue of Paulinus that was transferred from a site at Alnwick, and at the opposite side are two stone supports holding up an altar called the Holystone. Lady's Well is now in the care of the National Trust.

3 Follies

England's northern border country is renowned for sweeping expanses of moorland, dramatic coastal settings and many mighty fortresses. In this environment, it is perhaps not surprising to find so few neo-classical follies, but dotted around the county there is a series of Gothic-style structures. The momentum for this bout of folly building came from Hugh Percy Smithson, 1st Duke of Northumberland, during the second half of the eighteenth century. After employing James Paine and then the Adam brothers to restore and restyle Alnwick Castle, the Duke used the landscaping skills of Northumberland-born Lancelot 'Capability' Brown to mould adjacent parkland.

The most dramatic landscape feature is undoubtedly the Brizlee Tower, which crowns a 600ft hill on the northern perimeter. The spectacular Grade I listed structure was finished in 1781 and soars to a height of 80ft from a wide circular base composed of pointed arches and canopied niches. Rising from this central core, the main column has three storeys of pointed windows and niches topped by a battlemented octagon. The tower was most probably designed by the Adam brothers in 1777, although a fanciful tale suggested that it was modelled on a French cook's fabulous concoction in pastry. By the late 1990s Brizlee Tower was showing signs of a constant battering from the elements and in 2004 a major restoration scheme was begun to reinstate this glorious landmark.

While Brizlee Tower crowns a summit within Hulne Park on Alnwick's north-western fringe, a rather different structure dominates Ratcheugh Cliff some 2½ miles north-east of the castle. Ratcheugh observatory or gazebo spreads along the ridge above wooded slopes to form a dramatic range of single-walled buildings. Constructed in the mid-1780s as part of Robert and James Adam's ambitious scheme, it represents one of the finest imitation castle screens in the country. Openings on all sides of the structure led to its designation as a gazebo, and at the other end of a long screen of pointed arches and battlements a square tower offers fine views on all sides.

The Tenantry Column, which stands on high ground opposite Alnwick railway station, has links with the 2nd Duke of Northumberland and his tenant farmers. With a lion set on each corner of its square base, a fluted column soars 83ft to reach a drum that serves as a platform for a stately king of the jungle. It was designed by the architect David Stephenson and completed during 1816 for tenant farmers on the duke's estate. Following a devastating drop in agricultural prices at the end of hostilities in 1814 during the Napoleonic Wars, the duke

Brizlee Tower, completed in 1781, on the northern edge of the Duke of Northumberland's estate at Alnwick.

Ratcheugh observatory or gazebo, near Alnwick.

The Tenantry Column, known as the Farmers' Folly, at Alnwick.

had reduced their rents by 25 per cent and construction of the column was the farmers' way of demonstrating their appreciation for his benevolence. This statement of gratitude soon backfired, as the duke took their grateful gesture as an indication that they could afford to pay higher charges, and promptly restored them to the previous levels, hence the alternative title for the column – The Farmers' Folly.

During the 1760s Sir Walter Calverley Blackett of Wallington Hall employed the landscaping skills of 'Capability' Brown, but design work for mock castles was left to other architects. The rambling outlines of Rothley Castle, some 2 miles north of Scot's Gap, were completed during the mid-1750s from plans drawn up by Daniel Garrett. Some reports claim that it was intended to act as a defensive position during the Jacobite insurrection, but decorative features suggest that the emphasis was firmly placed on leisure pursuits. Pointed doors and windows as well as cross arrow slits added to the romance of this location during hunting forays.

Just over a mile away to the north another mock castle lines a ridge on the east side of the B6342. Known as Codger's Fort, it has a similar layout to Rothley

Codger's Fort, near Scots Gap.

Ford Castle's romanticised gateway.

Castle, but has rather less decorative detail in walls and end towers. Parts of Ford Castle, including the sturdy stone towers, date from the late thirteenth century and had to withstand attacks from Scottish forces during 1385, 1513 and 1549. Sir William Heron had been given a licence to crenellate his medieval fortress in 1338, but the dramatic features of the South and East Gates were added during much later bouts of romanticised rebuilding. It seems certain that Robert Adam was involved with Gothic-style additions during the early 1760s, and some thirty years later Alexander Gilkie added further embellishments to the gates and adjacent walls. The result is a wealth of architectural detail including quatrefoil openings, arrow slits, blind niches, castellations and a mock portcullis.

The slim, soaring outlines of Haggerston Tower dominate a popular holiday site close to the A1 in north Northumberland. Neo-Gothic in style, it was constructed in the mid-1890s as a lantern and water tower beside a large mansion. Other buildings on the site were demolished during 1933, but this incredible, lofty structure remains as an isolated and highly incongruous landmark.

A rather smaller tower occupies an elevated position in the hamlet of Whitton, South of Rothbury. During the early eighteenth century the archdeacon of Northumberland, Thomas Sharp, lived in an old pele tower in nearby Rothbury, and in an attempt to ease local unemployment levels he arranged for construction of an observatory. This circular building stands some 50ft high and included classical doorways and windows along with a battlement parapet.

In addition to its value as an observatory, Sharp's Folly offered splendid views across low ground to the distant coastline, but it soon fell into disuse. A restoration scheme during the early 1990s was largely unsuccessful with only a small plaque showing the date of construction.

Follies are dotted around the northern border landscape in a variety of shapes and sizes, but all have a unique story. The spreading outlines of Twizel Castle dominate the north bank of the River Till close to its confluence with the Tweed and have all the appearances of a genuine border stronghold. Yet the truth is rather different. Little is known about the mysterious ruin, apart from the fact

Sharp's Folly at Whitton, south of Rothbury.

that construction work began in the early 1770s and continued for some fifty years. This grand scheme was financed by Sir Francis Blake, who called in the architect James Nesbit and also employed George Wyatt about forty years into the project, but the building was never completed. Rising some five storeys in height, the walls remained a gaunt shell without floors and serve only as a monument to the extravagance and eccentricity of Sir Francis Blake.

A group of picturesque ruins is set in parkland around Blagdon Hall, south of Stannington village. Ranging from two open-roofed temple ruins to smaller Gothic style frontages, they date from the late eighteenth and early nineteenth centuries and were assembled by members of the Ridley family.

Another of Northumberland's notable families, the Delavals, created a number of buildings that were in keeping with their extravagant lifestyle (see chapter 10). Much of their wealth resulted from trading operations at Seaton Sluice where the 1st Lord Delaval re-routed the river channel through a rocky outcrop. The completed cut measured 52ft deep, 30ft wide and 900ft long.

Overlooking the harbour from the southern bank is 'the Octagon', a curious eight-sided building with muted Gothic-style windows. It probably served as the harbour master's office and almost certainly dates from the early 1760s when work on the harbour was completed.

'The Octagon' at Seaton Sluice overlooking the harbour.

Starlight Castle, overlooking Seaton Burn, was built as a wager by Sir John Delaval.

Kielder Castle, built in the 1770s for the 1st Duke of Northumberland.

Parkland around the family home at Seaton Delaval features the usual embellishments such as an obelisk and a mausoleum, but it is a hill-top ruin overlooking the nearby Seaton Burn that sums up the outrageous extravagance of this incredible family. Starlight Castle is a Gothic-style summer house, which was in all likelihood completed in one night time so that Sir John Delaval could win a wager. This inveterate gambler is said to have bet rivals that he could complete a castle during the hours of darkness. Unknown to them he had already prepared plans and materials so that this seemingly impossible scheme was firmly in place when morning broke.

Whereas the whimsical outlines of Starlight Castle resulted from a wager, there was a practical purpose beneath the fanciful stonework of Kielder Castle. It was built between 1772 and 1775 for the 1st Duke of Northumberland and served as a hunting lodge for the area around the confluence of North Tyne and Kielder Burn. Victorian additions cover the original battlemented frontage, but other sections of the eighteenth-century structure still have mock battlements, window supports and arrow loops.

From whole buildings to a small section of a structure, follies can be equally tantalising and attractive. Cockhall Folly at Eglingham (some 10 miles north-west of Alnwick on the B6346) is one end of a working farmhouse. Gothic-style features such as a triple-pointed arch window, obelisks and sloping battlements have been incorporated into its stonework.

4 A Coastline of Curiosities

The stretch of coastline between the Tyne and Tweed contains some of the most dramatic settings around mainland Britain. Harbours and coastal villages, islands, lighthouses and castles are set among sweeping beaches and bays. Leaving aside materials covering holy men (and women) as well as locations such as Berwick on Tweed and Bamburgh for inclusion in other chapters, there is a wealth of interest along this most dramatic of coastlines.

There are more than four hundred watermill sites between the two rivers with the earliest examples dating from the Roman period. A rare instance of an Anglo-Saxon watermill, with unusual horizontal waterwheel design, has been discovered near Corbridge, but the county's most intriguing corn mill is to be found on an exposed section of coastline at Scremerston, south of Berwick on Tweed. Standing on the edge of the beach, this small, ruinous mill building was designed by the notable civil engineer John Smeaton, and had a horizontal waterwheel similar to the one near Corbridge. A limited water supply and the bleak location influenced the design of this fascinating industrial relic that may well be unique in Britain.

In recent years small harbours along the Northumberland coastline have become an integral part of the area's tourist and leisure industry. Waterside locations attract visitors to vantage points for capturing coastal views, watching activity on fishing vessels or boarding boats for trips to offshore islands, but it is easy to overlook the scale and importance of earlier coastal trading activities.

A dramatic growth in agriculture during the mid-eighteenth century led to construction of turnpike roads, such as the Corn Road that linked inland market towns with Alnmouth. Seahouses never achieved the same importance as Alnmouth and Berwick in terms of agricultural exports, but granaries were built close to the harbour during the late eighteenth century, and between 1846 and 1847 a total of thirty-one vessels shipped more than 1,000 tons of grain from the harbour. A number of these, including the *Beadnell*, the *John* and *Constant Trader*, were operated by corn dealer John Railston, whose roadside home still stands in the nearby community of North Sunderland. Incoming cargoes often contained barrel staves, salt and iron hoops as well as building materials.

The only reminder of grain shipments from Seahouses is a set of properties at the southern end of Harbour Road. Built as granaries in the early 1820s, they were adapted as domestic dwellings later in the century and have been further

Seahouses harbour on the north Northumberland coast.

updated as holiday homes in recent years. Indications of the scale of lime burning in the area are more prominent as can be seen from a line of seven kilns at the northern end of Harbour Road, built in the 1770s. The upper section of each kiln was loaded with coal and limestone, which was then heated to a temperature of around 1,000°C. During this process lime dropped to the bottom of the kiln where it was cooled and loaded on ships moored at the old quay. Much of the cargo was transported to the Scottish towns of Perth and Dundee in 32- and 68-ton sloops. The processed lime was used as a fertiliser or in the manufacture of cement. The busiest period for the lime trade at Seahouses was during the 1830s and 1840s when shipments to Scotland took place almost every day during the summer months, but in the early twentieth century this industry was in serious decline.

The premises of Swallow Fish Ltd on South Street is the only remaining herring smokehouse in Seahouses. Along with herring sheds located on land on the north side of South Street these buildings formed the hub of the local herring fishing industry. Gangs of 'herring girls' prepared and packed the fish into barrels of brine that were shipped out of the harbour on small steamers and schooners heading for the ports of north Germany and Russia. These markets were lost after the First World War and the herring industry soon dwindled away with the tourist industry taking its place as the main employer in Seahouses. In the early

A fishing boat returning to Seahouses harbour.

Lime kilns on the harbour side at Beadnell.

twenty-first century crowds of visitors throng the harbour and approach roads largely unaware of the fascinating buildings and links with earlier industries that played such an important part in shaping the town.

Lime burning also played a major role in Beadnell's history. The discovery of a chapel on a rocky ridge along the north side of Beadnell Bay points to its Saxon origins, but it was during the mid-eighteenth century that the village enjoyed industrial expansion. Four kilns were completed on Delf Point by 1759, and the presence of nearby coal seams offered fine prospects for investors and workers through shipments of fish, lime and salt. Such developments required an improved harbour, and by 1798 a pier had been constructed. As herring fishing became more important than the lime trade harbour-side kilns were given over to herring curing, and Beadnell never achieved the anticipated levels of all-round trade. Later development took place a little distance inland close to the eighteenth-century Beadnell Hall, but the village's most curious feature must be the only west-facing harbour on the east coast of England.

Recent repair work has bolstered Beadnell harbour against ferocious North Sea breakers, but there is little trace of a much earlier harbour below the walls of Dunstanburgh Castle. Known as Queen Margaret's Cove, it is said to have been in use during the fifteenth century and, although access was difficult, King Henry

Beadnell harbour, the only west-facing harbour on the east coast.

Dunstanburgh Castle near Craster.

VIII's fleet sheltered there during 1514. The original scheme may have included measures to assemble a fortified port as an alternative to Berwick-upon-Tweed, but these plans were never completed and rock falls have blocked the entrance to the grassy hollow.

During the nineteenth century enterprising engineers prepared schemes to improve coastal navigation along England's east coast, and in 1883 Warkworth Harbour Commissioners drew up plans for a National Harbour of Refuge across the mouth of the River Coquet. With breakwaters reaching nearly 2 miles out to sea, it was to have included Coquet Island on the southern section. The workforce for this ambitious scheme would have been provided by convicts from a prison on the island, but it never got beyond the early planning stages.

Several of the prominent buildings in Alnmouth give clues to the township's early importance as a port. The buttressed walls of structures such as Hindmarsh Hall stored grain that was shipped to London and east coast ports of Scotland from the 1730s. Most vessels involved in the grain shipments were sloops or schooners and they usually returned with cargoes of soap, fuller's earth, wines and tobacco. During 1825–6 ten ships were based at Alnmouth, but the last commercial sailing ship left this small port in 1896. During a savage storm on Christmas Day 1806 North Sea breakers had forced a channel through the dunes and moved the course of the river to the north side of Church Hill, but this seems to have had little impact on trade. The emergence of Amble and the opening of the Newcastle and Berwick railway link in 1850 contributed to the decline of

Alnmouth Bridge carried the Corn Road to the harbour.

A probable guano store located on the coastal strip south of Alnmouth.

Alnmouth as a port. Grain shipments continued into the 1860s and timber was imported from northern Europe until the closing years of the nineteenth century, but trade had dwindled and virtually disappeared by time of the First World War. Alnmouth's recent prosperity has resulted from its popularity as holiday resort, but it is still possible to pick out former granaries which serve as a reminder of the town's prominent role in agricultural exports.

An intriguing building is located on the south side of Alnmouth among dunes overlooking the course of the old river channel. Constructed in brick and sandstone, this spreading single-storey structure shows signs of frequent rebuilding over the last two centuries. It is believed that one of its early functions was as a guano store. Guano (bird droppings) was imported on a large scale during the mid-nineteenth century when it was popular as a nitrogen fertiliser, and from the 1840s to the 1870s more than 12 million tons was transported to Britain from the Chincha Islands off the coast of Peru. Most shipments were landed at London, Bristol and Liverpool, and although there is no evidence that guano was brought directly to Alnmouth from South America, records from the mid-seventeenth century provide details of cargoes of fertilisers including kelp and guano. Documents from the 1870s show that up to sixteen boats each year shipped guano to the River Aln, but conclusive proof of this building's role as a guano store will only result from future environmental sampling within its ruined walls. Nowhere else in Britain is there an example of a guano shed from this

Launch of a concrete-built tug boat at Amble towards the end of the First World War.

period – a fact which only adds to the mystery surrounding this curious ruin. In 1988 it was scheduled as a building of national importance and given a Grade II listing.

Later uses of the guano shed are easier to identify. During the early stages of the Second World War windows were blocked and adapted as gun loops when the building became a pill-box. The extent of these rifle slits (20 in total) and other wartime alterations suggest that it may well have been at the heart of the defensive network for this stretch of the Northumberland coast.

During the First World War the Admiralty reacted to a shortage of steel by commissioning ships built from concrete. These unlikely vessels were constructed at a number of small shipyards including Whitby in North Yorkshire and Amble in Northumberland. The Amble yard was an offshoot of Messrs Palmer of Jarrow who had successfully pioneered the construction of colliers in iron during the nineteenth century, but concrete boats were rather less serviceable. Most of them were operated as tug boats or supply vessels, but a top speed of 4 knots restricted their value and they usually enjoyed a short operational life span.

The impressive stonework of Warkworth Castle is, in fact, composed of two castles. A conventional medieval castle took shape over many years with changes and adaptations to meet contemporary trends, but the second castle, namely the keep, was built to a single overall plan during the last two decades of the fourteenth century. While it is not unusual to come across double castles,

Warkworth Castle.

Warkworth bridge and tower.

The tower at the southern end of Warkworth Bridge.

Warkworth's keep has a very rare plan. Based on a square with a turret on each face, it is topped by a narrow look-out tower. (The south turret was renovated in the mid-nineteenth century to the designs of Anthony Salvin and the north turret displays a panel carved with the Percy lion). The cheerless ground-floor rooms were living quarters for pages and guards, while the first floor housed a hall, chapel and kitchen. Four separate staircases led to the second floor.

Warkworth has one of the very few fortified bridges in this country. A plain tower at the southern end of the two-arched bridge probably dates from the fourteenth century and gave an extra line of defence against attacks from the north.

Fear of invasion by German forces during the early months of 1940 led to an extensive network of defences throughout the country. In Northumberland lines of tank traps and gun emplacements were constructed along the coastline and these in turn were linked along waterways and railway routes to another system of defences which ran down the mainland's central spine. Pill-boxes were a feature of this network, and though many have been removed in recent years, it is still possible to trace a line of these defensive positions from Alnwick to Wooler, but the most curious surviving pill-box is located in Hemscott Hill Links between Widdrington and Cresswell. The small roofless building has gable ends and a chimney as well as gun loops, giving every appearance of a

Pill-box disguised as a bothy on Hemscott Hill Links between Widdrington and Cresswell.

Pill-box on Hemscott Hill Links
(side view).

converted farm cottage or bothy. In
fact, it was deliberately designed as a
pill-box with all round views across
Druridge Bay, though to invaders by
sea or air it would look like a genuine
rural dwelling. This rash of protective
systems ended in February 1942
when the emphasis was placed on
fluid defence with barbed wire, mines,
trenches and supporting infantry, but
this intriguing building survives as a
reminder of the early stages of the
Second World War when invasion
was seen as a very real prospect.

Further evidence of measures
intended to frustrate potential
invaders included obstacles positioned on beaches and open spaces
where enemy troop-carrying aircraft
or gliders might land. Over the
years most of these obstructions
have been removed, but on Beadnell
beach, where several old cars were
abandoned below the shoreline, one
skeletal vehicle occasionally emerges from the sands near the mouth of Long
Nanny Burn. The rusting frame is largely unrecognisable apart from a straight 4-
cylinder engine and wire-spoked wheels.

It is less than 2 miles from the relic of twentieth-century warfare at Hemscott
Hill to the ruined base of the oldest military religious order of Knights at Low
Chibburn near Widdrington. The Knights Hospitallers of St John of Jerusalem
were established in about 1048 and reached the mainland of Britain about
a hundred years later. With a base in London and support from secular and
religious leaders, their influence spread to other areas including the coast of
Northumberland, where Chibburn Preceptory comprised a group of buildings
enclosed by a moat. A chapel, tower and domestic quarters were probably
operated by both monks and nuns who catered for pilgrims journeying to and
from Lindisfarne. Following the closure of monastic properties under Henry
VIII the land passed to the Widdrington family, and during the mid-1550s they
adapted the layout to include an unusual cross passage dower house for widows.
Records indicate that Chibburn was attacked by a French raiding party in 1691.

Engraving of Blyth and harbour by William Alder.

Restoration work during 1995 uncovered evidence of adaptations to the buildings during the seventeenth and late nineteenth centuries and a Second World War gun loop in the chapel.

Lighthouses are quite a common sight around Britain's coastline, but it is not often that one is positioned in the middle of a public road. The High Light at Blyth was erected in 1788 to assist ships entering or leaving the nearby harbour and originally measured 40ft in height. It was raised to 54ft in 1888 and increased again to 61ft in 1901. During its first years of operation light was provided by a coal fire at the top of the tower; this was replaced by an oil lamp in the early nineteenth century. Further changes saw the installation of gas in 1857 and electricity during 1932 before its working days ended in the early 1980s. The line of properties that runs alongside the High Light formerly housed some of the town's most notable ship owners such as Thomas Knight and Robert Kell and dates from the late eighteenth century. Originally called Shiney Row, it was later re-named Paradise Row and more recently Bath Terrace.

Down the years the modern township of Blyth has caused an amount of consternation by its apparent lack of a recognised town centre. The reality is that contemporary Blyth is composed of two separate communities, South Blyth and Cowpen, with a muddy tidal beck, 'Blyth Gut', running down the middle. In the early nineteenth century the last of the stone bridges between the settlements was removed and the stream culverted under the road before joining the River

Blyth. The result was that Blyth acquired two distinct centres, one along Waterloo Road at Cowpen's market place and the other older one along Bridge Street, with notable public buildings such as the Custom House of 1890 and Lloyds Bank which was completed about ten years later.

There are a number of monastic houses in coastal settings along England's eastern seaboard, but it is unusual to find a monastery and castle interlinked on the same cliff-top location. Tynemouth's priory and castle stand on a rocky headland some 70ft about the confluence of the Tyne and North Sea with imposing ruins giving clues to a chequered history.

A monastery was founded on this cliff top during the seventh century, and it seems to have continued in use during the late ninth century despite destructive attacks by Danish raiding parties in 800, 865 and 870. It was re-established as a Benedictine priory during the late eleventh century by Robert de Mowbray and after a disagreement he transferred the dependence from Durham to St Albans. Written records indicate that recalcitrant monks were banished to this northern outpost where the biting winds and clinging sea mists no doubt taught them the error of their ways. During the early thirteenth century the chancel of the church was rebuilt to give the church a total length of about 260ft, and the rest of the 12-acre site was covered by monastic buildings on the south side with a dormitory to the east and farm buildings to the north. In times of peace the priory was self sufficient, but shortages during the Scottish wars hastened the construction of improved defences.

An aerial view of Tynemouth (including the castle and priory).

There is no trace of early medieval defensive features, but following a visit to this cliff-top location during the mid-1290s, King Edward I gave a licence to crenellate and strengthen the outer defences. Rebuilding of the curtain wall and towers seems to have been completed soon afterwards, but construction of the gatehouse, with adjoining barbican, dates from the period in office of Prior John de Whethamstede between 1393 and 1419. A sheltered area at the foot of the headland served as a harbour to supply the cliff-top community during troubled times.

In 1539 the priory was closed by Henry VIII's commissioners. Valuable items were removed and lands belonging to the priory disposed of, but the castle buildings were retained for military use. During 1544 Tynemouth was used as the base for an English fleet to invade Scotland, and Italian engineers carried out surveys to improve defensive fortifications. Further military positions were constructed in front of the gatehouse and another battery was set up on the other side of Prior's Haven. (It became known as the 'Spanish Battery' because at one time it was garrisoned by mercenaries from Spain.) Sir Thomas Hilton was commander at the fortifications up to his death in 1559 when he was replaced by Sir Henry Percy. Reports suggest that he found his term of office difficult, as Queen Elizabeth I attempted to cut the cost of maintaining fifty soldiers at the

Tynemouth priory and castle.

ROYAL MARINES

Wooden Dolly outside the
recruiting office, known
locally as Press Gang House.

Tynemouth base. The outcome was that Percy was fined for not maintaining the garrison properly and he died in prison during 1585. Robert Carey took over, and with the threat of a Spanish invasion in 1588 repairs were made to the fortifications. By the end of the sixteenth century the castle was again in a state of disrepair, and in 1605 the garrison's commander, the Earl of Northumberland, was drawn into events surrounding the Gunpowder Plot through his relative, Thomas Percy.

During the reign of James I successive commanders did little to repair the castle buildings, but this strategic position assumed more importance in the 1640s during the English Civil War. With the restoration of Charles II in 1660 Colonel Villiers was installed as captain of Tynemouth Castle, and during his time in charge some of the monastic buildings were converted to military use. Military positions have been maintained through to recent times. Gun emplacements were put in place in both world wars and the Tynemouth Artillery Volunteers, who were set up in 1859 to operate the castle guns, were only disbanded in 1959.

It is appropriate that a headland with such a rich military and church history should be the setting for a collection of fascinating gravestones. Notable among these is the headstone of Corporal Alexander Rollo of the Royal Artillery who died in 1856 at the age of eighty-two. His place in military history is assured as he held the lantern at the graveside during the burial of Sir John Moore at Corunna, in northern Spain, in 1809. The same graveyard was also the final resting place for two pre-conquest Kings, Oswin of Deira in about 651 and Osred of Northumbria in 792. Following his betrayal and assassination at Gilling, North Yorkshire, Oswin's body was buried at Tynemouth where his shrine drew large numbers of pilgrims.

While the outlines of Tynemouth's priory and castle give clues to the headland's chequered past, the nearby township of North Shields has a fascinating link with more recent history in the shape of a wooden dolly. The first in a series of dollies was a figurehead from the collier *Alexander and Margaret*, which was named after the ship's owners. Their son, David Bartleman, was fatally wounded while resisting attacks on his vessel *Fearnought* off Yarmouth in 1781. In 1814 the wooden dolly was positioned on Custom House Quay, but her attractive features counted for little among locals who eventually brought her tumbling down. Little is known about the second dolly, which stood in the same place for just over a decade from the mid-seventeenth century, but its successor, another figurehead, withstood rough treatment from locals until the early twentieth century. Among other indignities, the third dolly had to withstand the attention of sailors who punched holes in coins before nailing them to the landmark. The fourth dolly broke with tradition, for although she was placed on the same spot as her predecessors, the carved figure was depicted as a fishwife carrying a creel on her back. Two more dollies complete the series, with a fifth version in mahogany occupying a central position in Northumberland Square from 1958 and a final carving identical to the third dolly stationed outside the Prince of Wales on Custom House Quay since 1992.

5 Mighty Men and Incredible Beasts

Over the years the northern border country has produced endless tales of men with enormous strength as well as a whole collection of fascinating creatures. Local folklore has often exaggerated and embellished accounts of these incredible men and beasts, leaving the intriguing task of separating fact from fiction.

Often the mightiest local man was the village blacksmith, and this is true of Willie Carr who plied his trade at Hartley near Seaton Sluice. Born in 1750, he soon matured into a youth of immense proportions. At the age of seventeen he was said to stand 6ft 3in tall and weigh 16st. Everyday work in the smithy gave him the chance to develop his throwing and lifting skills, which he would then demonstrate at local fairs and social gatherings. Carr was a particular favourite at the extravagant parties that were staged by the Delaval family. Within the dramatic setting of Seaton Delaval Hall, he was pitted against champions from far and wide. When a prize fighter named Big Ben was brought to the hall from London reports suggest that Willie Carr was reluctant to fight and stated that he showed 'no ill will to the man'. His supporters eventually persuaded him to meet the challenger and Carr's response was to insist 'If we have to fight we must shake hands first'. Grasping Ben's fist, he is said to have screwed it like a vice and then crushed it until blood squirted from his fingertips. Big Ben was unwilling to continue and swore that he would 'prefer a kick from a horse to a blow from a fist such as Carr's'.

At another gathering at Seaton Delaval Hall, Lord Strathmore paraded a prize fighter named Mendoza to confront the Hartley giant, but after one look at the local champion's muscular frame, Mendoza beat a hasty retreat. As Willie Carr's reputation spread, so the myths sprung up about his amazing strength. He is said to have been able to lift a huge weight with either arm and regularly raised the Hartley Blue Stone that was later lodged outside the Delaval Arms. Another anecdote claims that he was able to carry a burly young girl under his arm while vaulting over a five-bar gate.

By the age of thirty Willie Carr stood 6ft 4in tall and weighed 30st, and when the press gang called at local ports he was an obvious potential recruit. Caught off guard, he was overpowered and transported to a ship in the nearby harbour, but Carr had no intention of leaving his home patch. According to reports, he propped his back against the stern and jammed his legs against the keel causing the boat to split apart, allowing him to swim ashore.

Later in life his skills as a blacksmith were directed into making harpoons for north-east whaling fleets. In order to supply one order on time Willie Carr is said to have worked non-stop for 132 hours, and on a different occasion he is reported to have transported a crate of harpoons on his back from Blyth to North Shields before drinking a total of 84 measures of gin on the return journey.

At the age of sixty Willie Carr was paralysed and he died several years later in 1825. A portrait of this giant of a man was commissioned by Lord Delaval and is now on display at Glamis Castle in Scotland.

A weathered statue on Palace Green at Berwick-upon-Tweed celebrates the life of local man, James Stuart, who was known in the district as 'Jimmy Strength'.

Percy's Cross at Otterburn, 1920.

56

The Battle of Hedgeley Moor information panel.

His prowess as a strong man was based on feats such as lifting a hay cart weighing 1½ tons, and he also achieved a measure of longevity. He died in 1844 at the age of 115 and was buried on the southern bank of the border river at Tweedmouth.

The border wars of the late medieval period provided any number of mercurial warriors, including several members of the Percy family. Sir Henry Percy, eldest son of the 1st Earl of Northumberland, was given the nickname 'Hotspur' supposedly because of the speed with which he attacked Scottish raiding parties. During the summer of 1388 James, Earl of Douglas, had plundered Northumberland and Durham before heading back towards his homeland. He delayed at Otterburn in order to ambush Hotspur's forces, and during the ensuing skirmish on a late August evening Douglas was cut down by Percy's sword. The spot is said to be marked by Percy's Cross, a vertical pointed column standing about 10ft high among a group of fir trees (after being moved from its original position in 1777 when the road was diverted). Hotspur was captured in the battle but survived to win a convincing victory at Humbleton Hill in 1403. Along with his father, Harry Hotspur played a major part in overthrowing Richard II in 1399, but when they later opposed Henry IV, Hotspur was killed at the Battle of Shrewsbury in 1403. The Percy family's extensive landholdings included territory on Tottenham Marshes in north London, so Hotspur was the name given to the local cricket team and in August 1882 to the football club.

The formidable Sir Ralph Percy led Lancastrian forces in the Battle of Hedgeley Moor, near Wooperton, against Yorkists under the command of John Neville. He

Percy's Leap at the site
of the Battle of Hedgeley
Moor.

was fatally injured during the fighting, but this redoubtable figure is immortalised by a cross and two moss covered stones. The stones, which are 9ft apart, are said to mark the length of the leap that Percy made after receiving the fatal wound. The 10ft high cross displays the stars and crescent of the Percy family and was probably erected by Sir Ralph's nephew, the 4th Earl of Northumberland.

Although their origins are unclear, it is believed that the herd of Chillingham wild cattle has been based on its current surroundings within Chillingham Park for some 700 years. It seems likely that they were taken from the large numbers of cattle that roamed freely in northern forests and contained within a perimeter wall to ensure a regular food supply. Close study of the skull and horns has indicated that they are direct descendants of the earliest ox on the British mainland, but reasons why they have stayed white are unclear.

The amazing longevity of these extraordinary beasts may be based on the fact that the fittest and strongest bull becomes 'king' and head of the herd. He

Chillingham village.

A herd of Chillingham wild white cattle, 1910.

continues as king as long as he remains unbeaten in combat, and during his period of leadership he will sire all calves that are born. This process guarantees that only the best available blood line is carried forward. When a bull wishes to challenge the king he will leave the herd and begin to bellow and paw the ground. If the challenge is accepted, the leader will also move away from the herd and face the challenger from a few yards away. In due course, and quite unexpectedly, one of the bulls will attack, but after a confrontation lasting as little as half a minute both beasts will continue grazing while maintaining a wary eye on the opponent in the hope of catching him off guard. This sequence of events continues until one of the bulls seems to accept defeat. The loser moves away into temporary exile, where he remains cantankerous and extremely dangerous to approach. Other lesser combats between bulls and even between cows and their sons are believed to represent a sort of 'training exercise'.

During the inter-war period the size of the herd remained fairly even at between thirty-five and forty animals, but numbers were dealt a severe blow in the savage weather of spring 1947. Supplies of hay were already low when the park was hit by snowdrifts of up to 40ft in depth, and during the ensuing shortage of hay and straw, twenty cattle died, leaving eight cows, five bulls and no young beasts. Fears that the herd might face extinction were eased when a healthy calf was born in August 1948, and since then numbers have gradually increased. The other major threat to the future of the herd has come with outbreaks of foot and mouth disease in 1967 and 2001, which prompted the establishment of a small reserve herd in Scotland.

The wild nature of the cattle dictates a particular approach to care and feeding. They will only eat meadow hay and occasionally straw. Supplies are spread in open ground and at a different location every day in order to keep them moving and on clean ground. The undomesticated nature of the cattle also means that it is not feasible to provide any sort of veterinary support at times of disease or during calving. Cows give birth to their calves away from the rest of the herd, and for the first week or more the calves are hidden among undergrowth. Anyone approaching during this period will be attacked by the mother. Eventually the calf is introduced to the herd, and as cow and calf head towards the others, the king bull will approach and then escort them for inspection by the herd. A process of inspection follows, and if the calf is accepted it remains unnoticed among the herd.

In 1939 the Chillingham Wild Cattle Association took over care and maintenance of the herd from Lord Tankerville, and on his death in 1971 they assumed ownership. The future of the herd was also put in doubt with the death of 9th Earl of Tankerville in 1980. A decision was taken to sell the Chillingham estate, but with direction from the Duke of Northumberland the park and woodlands were bought by the Sir James Knott Charitable Trust. The trust soon granted the association a new lease of the grazing rights for 999 years, and consequently guaranteed the future of the wild cattle at Chillingham.

Bamburgh Castle, linked with the tale of the Laidley Worm at Spindlestone Heugh.

The so-called Bamburgh Beast was uncovered in 1971 during excavations to the north of the keep.

With its dramatic historical background and impressive setting Bamburgh Castle is inevitably linked with several monster stories. A ballad called 'The Laidley Worm of Spindlestone Heugh' is said to be based on old Northumbrian tales, although it seems likely that most of it was composed by the writer the Revd Robert Lambert of Norham. According to his account a king brought a new wife to Bamburgh whose jealousy for his daughter caused the girl to be turned into a Laidley Worm, a horrible serpent or dragon. From her den at the base of Spindlestone Heugh, she demanded a daily delivery of milk from seven cows into a nearby trough and breathed poisonous fumes across the adjacent countryside.

Stories about the loathsome beast reached 'Childy Wynd', heir to the Bamburgh lands, who set sail for these northern shores. In spite of the wicked queen's attempt to prevent them from landing, Childe's party reached Budle Sands and set out for the monster's lair. As he approached she called out to him to reverse the curse by giving her three kisses, and when he did this she turned out to be his sister. Their next move was to challenge the wicked queen, and by reversing her own spell they changed her into a hideous toad. Local tradition states that she was still living in the cave near Bamburgh Castle in the late nineteenth century and would not be released from the spell until she was kissed three times. The story has strong links with other early ballads, and although the Laidley Worm's cave was quarried away by the end of the nineteenth century, Spindlestone Heugh is shown on modern Ordnance Survey maps.

A painting within Bamburgh Castle's museum illustrates the legend of the Laidley Worm; other fiendish creatures are also featured there. During 1971 archaeologists involved in excavation work at the north end of the castle precincts unearthed a small item of beautifully worked gold. It was no larger than a thumbnail and dated from the early seventh century. A design worked into the metal featured an intertwined beast, which gave rise to its name, 'the Bamburgh Beast'. Excavations continued to a depth of 8ft and found evidence of human habitation spreading back some 1,600 years. A later survey team in 1998 used ultrasonic scanning equipment to discover evidence of man-made fortifications pre-dating the Roman occupation of Britain.

Dunstanburgh, another of Northumberland's coastal castles, has a legend involving a beautiful young maiden and a secret cavern. According to the folk tale, a knight named Guy the Seeker arrived during a stormy night seeking shelter at Dunstanburgh Castle. He was challenged by a wizard to rescue the maiden who had been bewitched in the cavern. After taking up the challenge, Guy followed the wizard along a dark winding stairway until they reached a large bolted door that was guarded by a poisonous snake. The courageous wizard dispatched the snake and opened the doorway into a huge darkened chamber. At the far end lay the beautiful young maiden sleeping in a tomb of crystal which was guarded by two malevolent skeletal figures. The skeleton on the right held a falchion (broad sword) and the one on the left held a horn. According to the wizard, the girl's destiny depended on the knight's choice of the horn or sword

THE WOLF HUNT

HUNTER AND FARMERS CAN'T AGREE AS TO TERMS.

Visited by a "Northern Echo" reporter yesterday, Mr. W. Briddick stated that the negotiations between himself and the Hexham farmers had broken down.

"Why?" asked our reporter.

"Read these wires," said Mr. Briddick, "and they will explain."

The first, as the others, was from Mr. John Balden, Stocksfield-on-Tyne, and read. "Will you, Mr. Briddick, undertake to kill the wolf, no public hunting allowed; state terms."

Mr. Briddick's answer was: "I will undertake to kill wolf, kill or no kill expenses, wolf to be my property."

Mr. Balden replied: "Do you insist on wolf becoming your property, as committee think the same should be at the disposal of Mr. Balden?"

Mr. Briddick replied: "Wolf to be my property, expenses kill or no kill; this is definite."

Then came the final word: "Committee thank you for your offer, but cannot accept."

Mr. Briddick says he asks no more than what is right, when asking for the wolf. "However," said the hunter, "they have

A newspaper article referring to the Wolf Hunt on 21 December 1904.

and after choosing to blow the horn Sir Guy is said to have fallen into a deep sleep. When he awoke the knight found himself outside the castle in the midst of the storm, and although he spent the rest of his life attempting to re-discover the cave, his search was in vain.

King Arthur and the Knights of the Round Table feature in legends up and down the country, including Sewingshields Crag on Hadrian's Wall, where they are said to lie sleeping in a cave. A shepherd supposedly discovered the cave entrance and followed a trail of thread along the tunnel towards the underground cavern. As he approached the slumbering knights the shepherd sounded a horn which caused the warriors to stir and sent him scrambling for the way out. It is claimed that he spent the rest of his days trying to find the place again.

Giant's Grave lies close to the modern village of Rudchester some 10 miles west of Newcastle. It is a moss-covered basin cut in solid rock and measures 12ft in length, 4ft 6in across and 2ft deep with a hole near the bottom of one end. Discovered in 1766, the Giant's Grave was found to contain numerous bones and an iron implement. Local lore suggests that it was used by the Romans for making beer from bell heather, and another theory which claims that it was part of a temple to the Persian sun god, Mithras, is supported by the nearby discovery of altars in 1844.

Wolves disappeared from the remote parts of Britain several hundred years ago, but memories of these feared beasts was revived in 1904 when sheep flocks in the Allendale area were savaged by a lone wolf. Daniel Defoe had reported packs of wolves howling when he stayed at Bewcastle, some 30 miles away from Allendale, in the late eighteenth century, and fears were raised that survivors of those packs were again running loose. Hunters set out to track down the lone wolf, but their guns stayed silent, for the so-called Allendale wolf strayed on to the railway track near Carlisle and was struck by a train. It transpired that the young male, which measured 5ft in length, had escaped from a private zoological garden outside Consett, County Durham.

6 Puzzles in Stone, Turf and Timber

At first sight Northumberland's spreading moorland expanses give little indication of the range of earlier human activity in these remote locations. Yet among the heather-covered slopes and rocky outcrops lies evidence that early settlers lived, worked and worshipped at these isolated settings. The nature and purpose of some features has been clearly identified, but others have attracted a wealth of folklore and remain shrouded in mystery.

Numerous tales are linked with the landscape around Simonside, some 4 miles south of Rothbury. In recent years forestry schemes have covered over numerous burial sites that take the form of mounds or cairns above a cavity containing cremations. A number of these locations were investigated during the late Victorian era, and records were compiled by archaeologists such as David Dixon. The discovery of items such as flint tools and earthenware pots have been dated to the early Bronze Age (about 2,000 BC).

In the depths of forest on the northern slope of Simonside stands a remote outcrop of sandstone known as Little Church Rock. A narrow cavern on one side of the huge boulder has room for up to eight people, whose illegal services may have given the rock its name. Towards the lower side of the rock it is possible to make out a group of cup marks that may be the result of natural weathering or could well be Stone Age inscriptions.

At a higher level on the wooded northern slope a huge rock juts out over the track offering a sheltered refuge for travellers. Speculation suggests that this rocky haven has been used for generations, but no firm evidence of human occupation has so far been uncovered.

Just below the rock shelter the track narrows and crosses a level sandstone slab that has sets of carved lines worked into the surface. No one can point with any certainty to the origins of marks on the flat stone. They may date from the Stone Age or could have been cut some two or three centuries ago when this route was a well-used drover's road for cattle being moved to markets further south. The grooves on the rock could have been scored in the surface to provide livestock with a firmer footing as they were herded along the slope.

Little more than a mile to the east of Simonside's slopes lies the open moorland of Lordenshaws, where evidence of human occupation stretches back some

Cup and ring marks at Lordenshaws.

More cup and ring marks at
Lordenshaws.

6,000 years. Rock carvings, which
are collectively known as 'cup and
ring marks', are made up of cup
marks, rings and interlinking chan-
nels. These are best seen close to
the western edge of the moor. The
possible significance and origins of
the carvings continue to generate
much debate, with possible explanations ranging from maps to fertility
symbols, while the arrangement of
the carved rocks may be linked with
routes and viewpoints.

In January 2005 archaeologists
completed a survey of Northumberland's moorland areas and
included around 250 cup and ring
sites on a new website. Experts
from the University of Newcastle
discovered new sites including a
collection at Goatstones, near Wark,
where fourteen carved stones were
located. It is now believed that they
were the work of Neolithic and Early Bronze Age people who lived in these
remote areas between 6,000 and 3,500 years ago. Much of the research has
centred around the findings of Dr Stan Beckensall, who has devoted more than
thirty years to documenting these amazing rock features.

Southern moorland slopes at Lordenshaws have numerous low heaps of stones
topped by turf which probably represent successive farmers' attempts to clear
stones from areas under the plough. No firm date has been attached to these
cairnfields, though other similar features are believed to date from the Bronze
Age. On the north-eastern side of the Iron Age hillfort there are stones of a
rather different nature. Large stone slabs have been arranged to form graves or
cists where the body would have been placed beneath a central capstone. These
burial mounds have been identified as dating from the Early to Middle Bronze
Age, some 4,000 to 3,000 years ago.

The highest sector of the Lordenshaws moor marks the site of an impressive
Iron Age hillfort. Sunken roadways from the east and west sides run through a
defensive layout of banks and ditches to the central area. Building work on the

Cup and ring stone at Ingram.

fort complex probably began in about 350 BC and there is evidence of two stages in construction of the defences. Later adaptations of the ramparts appear to have been carried out to accommodate round stone houses on the south-east sector and farming land on the north and east side.

Other features on the Lordenshaws landscape indicate changing use of the countryside. The boundary bank from the thirteenth-century deer park extends for about 3 miles around the moor, and close to the hill fort it is possible to trace medieval rig and furrow farmland. Hollow workings on the east side of the hill fort probably represent an unsuccessful attempt to uncover veins of lead in the early nineteenth century, while the foundations of rectangular properties are thought to have been shielings used by shepherds since the medieval period.

There is a touch of the wild west frontier days at Stonehaugh, near Wark, where a set of three elaborately carved totem poles dominate open ground close to the village. Plans were made after the Second World War for eight new villages to house workers at the extensive forests along the North Tyne valley. The architect for the overall scheme was Thomas Sharp. His original plans for Stonehaugh included 158 houses, 2 churches, 2 pubs, 5 shops, a school and a village hall. When work finally began in 1951 the scheme had been drastically modified with only three villages to be constructed.

Stonehaugh was reduced from 158 houses to only 35 with none of the amenities that were first planned, but there was no shortage of workers when

Three carved totem poles at Stonehaugh, near Wark.

wages were £6 2s per week. The first residents arrived during snowy weather in February 1954, and some soon returned to urban settings on Tyneside, but within a year Stonehaugh gained a village hall, in the form of a hut from the former Italian prisoner of war camp at Kielder. It soon became the focal point for a whole range of social activities ranging from dances to darts matches. This tiny community survived harsh winters in the late 1950s and early 1960s and in many ways the totem poles seem to sum up the spirit of Stonehaugh. In fact, the current poles are the third set on this site. The first poles were carved by two local craftsmen in 1970 and the second set was removed for safety reasons when their bases began to deteriorate.

John and Benjamin Green, architects and engineers, were based in Newcastle during the mid-nineteenth century during a period of rapid industrialisation. They designed several buildings and bridges throughout the north-east, including Newcastle's Theatre Royal and Whorlton Bridge across the Tees, near Barnard Castle. The Newcastle and North Shields Railway was completed in 1839 and included two unusual viaducts at Willington and Byker. Both structures were assembled with a laminated timber arch designed to the Wiebeking system. The Ouseburn viaduct has five spans at a height of 108ft above the foundations and with a total length of 918ft. The timber arches were replaced by iron ones in 1869 and the viaduct was widened to carry four tracks in 1885. The Willington

Limestone rock formation in Kielder forest.

viaduct has seven spans at a height of 82ft and it was also rebuilt with ironwork arches in 1869.

These two viaducts are widely regarded as the earliest laminated timber-arch railway bridges in Britain, and there is evidence that the Green brothers planned to cross the Tyne with a similar structure. Many viaducts in the early years of railway building included timber superstructures of various types, and laminated arches were favoured by many engineers after the success of Willington and Ouseburn.

Cambo church dates from the early 1840s and has a tower which was added in 1884. It has some fine Victorian glasswork honouring members of the Trevelyan family from nearby Wallington and a collection of medieval grave covers built into walls on the west end of the church. The interior is high and its lofty roof timbers represent the only surviving example of John Green's use of timber laminate, where beams were made by binding layers together.

Among the scattered rocky outcrops on Northumberland's moorland wastes are a number of man-made monuments with religious or territorial significance. Historians can often provide indications about their origins, but most sites retain an amount of mystery and intrigue. A group of early British grave mounds at Cheviot Farm, near Hallington, provide proof of human occupation in this area, but the most prominent feature is the Swinburn standing stone. It rises to a height of almost 12ft from the centre of a field on the south side of Swinburn Castle and is regarded as the most impressive prehistoric monolith in Northumberland. Underneath a covering of grey lichen the stone has a reddish hue, and although the deep grooves in the top have probably been caused by weathering, a vertical face has curious cup markings as well as a number of modern initials.

A row of standing stones is spread for about 16yds across ground near Holystone. Collectively known as The Five Kings, their heights range from 5 to 8ft and four of the series remain upright. A single limestone column stands to a height of about 7ft in a roadside field between Branxton and Cornhill and is known as the King's Stone. Experts point to prehistoric origins for this prominent monolith.

The summit of a mound near Newton (close to Chillingham) is topped by the shaft of an Anglican cross. It stands some 13ft high and is believed to be contemporary with the well-known eighth-century cross at Bewcastle, although its socket was fashioned in 1838.

South of Otterburn, a pathway leads from Old Town Farm to a boggy area of ground with the delightful name of Silver Nut Well. In earlier days the bubbling waters used to bring up to the surface parts of forest trees and perfectly preserved hazel nuts with a silvery coating caused by a chemical reaction. Some of these strange subterranean curiosities were bottled and sold. The well also attracted an amount of folklore, which suggests that a horse and cart filled with hay was engulfed by the seething waters.

The crypt of Hexham's priory church was completed by Wilfred in about 680 and incorporates Roman stonework showing decoration and inscriptions. Other sectors of the church were destroyed in Danish raids during 876 and it was reformed as the church of a priory of Augustinian Canons in 1113. Most of the present building dates from the periods 1180 to 1250, and 1850 to 1910. The medieval phase illustrates aspects of the Early English style of architecture along with some fascinating items of woodwork. Choir stalls are mainly fifteenth century and the misericords show fine carvings of fanciful heads, roses and pelicans feeding their young. The chancel screen dates from the time of Thomas Smithson, who was prior from 1491 to 1524, and its magnificent woodwork is rated as some of the finest in England. On the north side of the sanctuary is the chantry chapel of Prior Rowland Leschman, who died in 1491. There are contrasts in stonework at the lower level and more detailed woodwork at the higher sections. This is probably best seen in oak screen work with its intricate ornamental outlines and the cruder carvings along the bottom. A rather more prominent item of stonework is the Frith Stool or Sanctuary Chair, where fugitives from the law could claim the church's protection. This area of safety was later extended to a mile around the building with the limits indicated by stone crosses.

7 A Collection of Clerics and Caring Places

Northumberland's sweeping landscapes are dominated by dramatic castle buildings at locations such as Warkworth, Bamburgh, Alnwick and Norham, and amid the echoes of mighty warriors and border conflicts it is easy to overlook the importance of churchmen in this area's early history.

Paulinus was born in about AD 563 in Italy and left for England in 601. He was sent by Pope Gregory the Great to assist Augustine with his missionary work in southern areas of the country but in 625 he moved to northern parts. King Edwin of Northumbria was still a pagan, and there are dramatic reports about the conversion of leading nobles at a meeting that was probably held in the East Yorkshire village of Londesborough. The king himself was soon baptised at York (on Easter Day, 12 April 627) with two of his children and other leaders.

Edwin's kingdom covered territory between the Rivers Humber and Clyde, and there are references to Paulinus's ministry in many parts of the area. According to the writings of Bede, he baptised converts in the Swale, near Catterick, and also had links with Easingwold, Leeds and Dewsbury. Further north (in Northumberland) there are connections with Pallinsburn and St Paulinus' Well, also known as the Lady's Well, Holystone. Paulinus is said to have baptised around 3,000 people at this tranquil location in 627. (During the early fifth century this setting was known as St Ninian's Well, which suggests a link with the early Scottish missionary.) A second well, situated opposite Holystone's church, is named after St Mungo, who probably passed this way on his journeys from St Asaph, in Wales, to Glasgow.

Edwin of Northumbria had a base at Yeavering, at the foot of the Cheviots, and it was here that Paulinus is said to have spent thirty-six days instructing converts before baptising them in the nearby River Glen. Following the death of Edwin at the Battle of Hatfield Chase in 633, Paulinus returned to Kent and died there some eleven years later.

Oswald was born in the early seventh century and spent much of his early life in Scotland and Northern Ireland. It was during this period that he was converted to Christianity and baptised on Iona before returning to Northumbria. After deposing Cadwalla, Oswald ruled the kingdom for eight years before he was killed in battle against Penda of Mercia. In addition to his prowess as a warrior,

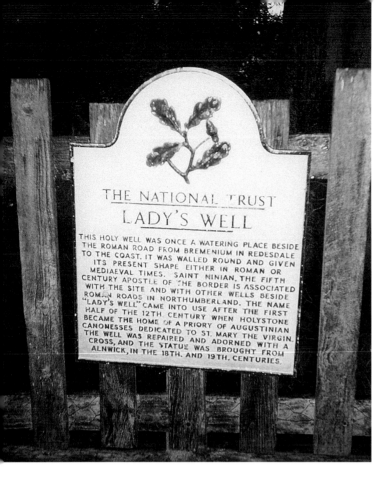

Holystone, where Paulinus is said to have baptised around 3,000 people in 627.

St Aidan is said to have died at Bamburgh, probably on a visit to the royal court, on 31 August 651.

Oswald gained a reputation as a pious Christian monarch who played a major role in establishing Christianity in the north of England. Soon after becoming king he established a bishopric on Holy Island, and he is acknowledged with devoting much of his time to prayer and meditation. According to the writings of Bede, King Oswald was dining with Aidan and other officials on Easter Day, but left the banquet to distribute his food and a silver dish to a crowd of paupers who had gathered outside. Following his death in 642, Oswald's head, arms and hands were severed by his enemies only for them to be recovered by his brother and displayed in churches at Lindisfarne and Bamburgh. Locations linked with Oswald were soon credited with miraculous powers of healing, and he became regarded as one of the foremost royal saints of Anglo-Saxon England.

Aidan was sent from Iona to Northumbria in 635 after a previous missionary had failed to make an impact on King Oswald's followers. He spent the next sixteen years organising the Christian church by setting up religious centres on land provided by members of the aristocracy. Working closely with members of the ruling classes, Aidan was an influential figure at royal courts, particularly at Bamburgh where he worked closely with Oswald. He also valued the importance of education and set up a school for Northumbrian boys, whose pupils included St Chad. These trainees were instrumental in establishing monastic centres in the north country.

Lindisfarne Priory from the churchyard.

Aidan carried his Christian beliefs into his daily life and followed principles of poverty and charity by using funds to assist the poor and ransom slaves. On one occasion it is claimed that King Oswin gave Aidan a horse for his own use to travel around the countryside during his ministry of preaching and baptising. When a poor man approached and asked for alms, Aidan dismounted and handed over the horse to the beggar. Oswin's objections to his generosity were met by a swift rebuttal, and it seems that Aidan was outspoken in his criticisms of wrongdoers with regard to their status.

King Oswin was murdered by supporters of King Oswiu of Bernicia, and just twelve days later, probably during a visit to the royal court at Bamburgh, Aidan became ill. He sheltered beside the west wall of the church and died there on 31 August 651 with his head resting against a post that served as a buttress. The timber church was twice destroyed by Viking raiders, but on each occasion the post incredibly survived intact. During his lifetime Aidan was credited with miraculous powers, including redirecting the wind away from the royal base at Bamburgh during an attack by Penda, King of Mercia, and chippings from the timber beams were credited with healing properties.

A doorway at Lindisfarne Priory.

Aidan was buried at Lindisfarne, but some of his remains were removed to Iona by Bishop Colman after the Synod of Whitby in 664. Other relics of Aidan seem to have survived Viking raids in the late eighth century before being moved to Glastonbury Abbey in Somerset.

It is believed that Cuthbert was born into a noble Northumbrian family in about 634. Following contemporary practice, he was placed in the care of a foster mother from the age of eight and then spent some time as a soldier. After the death of Aidan in 651, Cuthbert is said to have been inspired by a vision of angels carrying his soul to heaven, and this influenced him to join the monastery at Melrose.

He soon gained status through his devout nature and capacity for learning, and in about 661 he went to Ripon as guest master. Roman Catholic practices were adopted at Ripon, but Cuthbert chose to return to Melrose where the customs of Celtic Christianity were followed. An outbreak of plague struck the community at Melrose, but Cuthbert survived and was appointed prior in place of St Boisil.

From this base he spent periods preaching in surrounding areas, and was often away for up to a month at a time. Following the Synod of Whitby, Cuthbert was appointed prior of Lindisfarne, but in 676 he left the monastery to pursue a life of solitude on Inner Farne. He adopted traditional Irish monastic practices of solitude and hardship, building a hermitage from stones and turf, which included a room for prayer as well as domestic areas. He reputation as a wise counsellor meant that clerics and royalty sought his guidance. On one occasion he warned Ecgfrith against invading Ireland, but the attack went ahead. Following Ecgfrith's death at Nechtansmere, Cuthbert left Inner Farne to meet Aelfflaed on Coquet Island, near Amble, where the main topic in their discussions was the return of Aldfrith.

In 685 he was elected Bishop of Lindisfarne, but as his health deteriorated Cuthbert returned to his cell on the Farne Islands at Christmas 686. He died in March 687 and was buried in the monastery at Lindisfarne. Soon after his death Cuthbert's tomb was linked with cures, forecasts and angelic visions as the stone-lined grave became a place of pilgrimage. During the Danish invasion of 875 Bishop Eardulf and the monks fled from Lindisfarne taking the body of St Cuthbert with them as they travelled through Cumberland and southern Scotland. In 883 the body was kept in a church at Chester le Street, but a century later fears of another attack caused it to be moved to Ripon for a few months. It was then returned to Durham until William I's attack on the north country in 1069 caused its removal to Lindisfarne. From 1104 Cuthbert's shrine was transferred to the present cathedral, and by the time it was ransacked in 1542 the saint's body had been moved to a secret location. It is alleged that this hiding place is known to a small number of Benedictine monks who pass on details from one generation to another.

A measure of Cuthbert's importance can be seen in the numerous churches, monuments and crosses that have been erected in his honour, as well as other

Dunstanburgh cliffs contain crinoid skeletons, which became known as St Cuthbert's beads.

locations and creatures linked with the saint. St Cuthbert's Cave is a natural shelter near Holburn (some 3 miles north-west of Belford). One theory suggests that Cuthbert spent time here in solitude before moving to the Farne Islands, but another version claims that monks fleeing from Viking raiders rested at this location with the saint's body. Carvings on nearby rocks are memorials to previous owners of the cave, which is now in the care of the National Trust.

Another legend states that Cuthbert had kneeled to pray on the tiny St Cuthbert's Island, to the south of Holy Island, when he was almost overcome by the inrushing tide. Salt water allegedly rotted the cord of his rosary causing the beads to fall into the sea. Though they are rarely found nowadays St Cuthbert's beads were traditionally gathered by religious pilgrims in order to fashion rosaries. The truth is that large numbers of crinoids, brachiopods and corals lived in the warm shallow waters which covered this area of Northumberland. When they died these primitive creatures fell to the bottom of the sea and formed layers of sediment which hardened into rock deposits. Crinoid skeleton joint sections have the appearance of beads, and although they are not often found on the beaches of Holy Island, they do occur in limestone cliffs on the island's north shore.

Hexham Abbey was constructed by St Wilfred.

St Wilfred's Gate, Hexham.

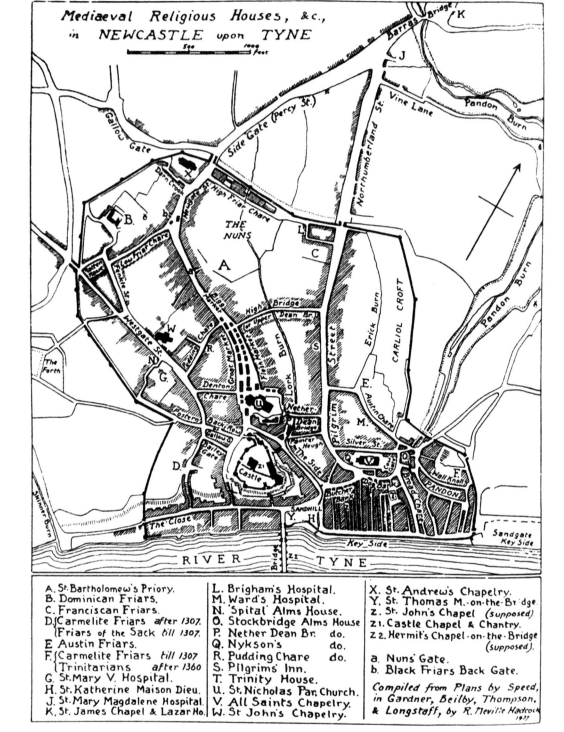

Mediaeval Religious Houses, &c., in NEWCASTLE upon TYNE

A. St. Bartholomew's Priory.	L. Brigham's Hospital.	X. St. Andrew's Chapelry.
B. Dominican Friars.	M. Ward's Hospital.	Y. St. Thomas M.-on-the-Bridge.
C. Franciscan Friars.	N. 'Spital' Alms House.	z. St. John's Chapel (supposed).
D. Carmelite Friars after 1307. Friars of the Sack till 1307.	O. Stockbridge Alms House	z1. Castle Chapel & Chantry.
	P. Nether Dean Br. do.	z2. Hermit's Chapel-on-the-Bridge.
E. Austin Friars.	Q. Nykson's do.	(supposed).
F. Carmelite Friars till 1307 Trinitarians after 1360	R. Pudding Chare do.	a. Nuns' Gate.
	S. Pilgrims' Inn.	b. Black Friars Back Gate.
G. St. Mary V. Hospital.	T. Trinity House.	Compiled from Plans by Speed,
H. St. Katherine Maison Dieu.	U. St. Nicholas Par. Church.	in Gardner, Beilby, Thompson,
J. St. Mary Magdalene Hospital.	V. All Saints Chapelry.	& Longstaff, by R. Neville Hadcock
K. St. James Chapel & Lazar Ho.	W. St. John's Chapelry.	1937

Medieval religious houses in Newcastle.

Blackfriars buildings, Newcastle.

Blackfriars, Newcastle.

Cuthbert has also been described as one of the world's first wildlife conservationists. Many of the accounts about him include animals such as an eagle and several otters, and he is said to have protected the eider duck, which is also known as St Cuthbert's duck (or locally around Lindisfarne as 'Cuddy's duck').

Wilfred was born in about 634 into a Northumbrian aristocratic background, and at the age of fourteen decided to take up the religious life at the monastic school on Holy Island. During 652 he was accompanied on a visit to Rome by Benedict Biscop, and on the return journey Wilfred stopped at Lyons to take his monastic vows. His close links with the royal family of Northumbria and an exceptional increase in landholdings and wealth resulted in a tempestuous series of events during the late seventh century. He was stripped of his living as a bishop on three occasions, and when he was finally restored in 706 the size of his diocese had been reduced to an area linked to his monastery at Hexham. In spite of these tribulations Wilfred made impressive contributions to the early church in

Carmelite Friary (far right), Newcastle.

Holy Jesus Hospital, opened in 1681.

Keelmen's Hospital, opened in 1701.

Northumbria. He instigated impressive building schemes at Ripon, Hexham and York and established the Rule of St Benedict in Northumbria, as well as carrying out missionary work during his periods of office.

With such a collection of influential Northumbrian churchmen, it is perhaps not surprising that Newcastle was the setting for a considerable number of religious houses from the early medieval period. By the late twelfth century there were already four churches within the settlement that covered about 150 acres. St Nicholas' was a parish church within the diocese of Durham until 1882 (when Newcastle became a cathedral city). The original building was destroyed by fire in 1248 and most of the present structure has a fourteenth-century interior and fifteenth-century exterior. The splendid crown spire soars almost 200ft skywards and was the gift of a Newcastle merchant Robert Rhodes. All Hallows Church could accommodate a congregation of up to 2,000 and served the quayside area, but by 1780 it had fallen into a state of disrepair and was replaced on the same site by All Saints'. St Andrew's Church probably represents the oldest religious house in Newcastle, with a west tower built in the late twelfth century reusing Roman stonework, while St John's present structure dates from the fifteenth century.

At one time there were no fewer than five friaries within Newcastle's walls, but the only notable remains are at Blackfriars. After the closure of monastic houses during the 1530s the friary was bought by the mayor and burgesses of the town and subsequently leased to nine different trade guilds. The chapel and hospital of St Thomas the Martyr was located at the northern end of the modern Tyne Bridge. The first documentary reference appears in 1248, and the master of the hospital also served as keeper of the medieval bridge. The hospital of St Mary the Virgin was operating by 1190 and had premises close to the modern Stephenson monument at the bottom of Westgate Road.

In addition to this proliferation of churches and religious houses, Newcastle has a long-standing tradition of care for the sick. In 1752 public subscriptions paid for a general infirmary at Forth Banks. Land for the building was provided by the corporation at a minimal rent. Some eight years later, in 1760, a lying-in hospital was set up on Rosemary Lane (close to St John's Churchyard).

Wesley Orphan House, Newcastle.

The Holy Jesus Hospital opened in 1681 'for the maintenance, sustenation and relief of poor people being Freeman or Freemen's widows'. It stood on the site of a building used by the Austin friars and included three storeys with an attractive piazza and fountain. Inmates were given an allowance of £4 per year, but this was later increased to £6 and latterly £13. During the nineteenth century another building was added to accommodate welfare work, but the property closed in 1937 and remained empty for some years. It was saved from possible demolition and adopted as the John George Joicey Museum (in honour of the Gateshead coal owner who had funded the initial scheme).

The Keelmen's Hospital was opened in 1701 to provide accommodation for poor, old or disabled keelmen and their widows. Funds for this imposing building were raised by the keelmen themselves, and the completed structure included a raised entry at the foot of a central tower that incorporates a sundial and clock. During the early nineteenth century the adjacent area was populated by shipwrights, watermen and seafarers, but the development of staithes and dredging of the Tyne led to the decline of this workforce. By 1872 the Society of Keelmen had been abolished, but the Keelmen's Hospital remains (as student accommodation) and serves as a dramatic reminder of the spirit of care and support that spread across Newcastle from medieval times.

8 Landmarks and Intriguing Locations

From dramatic industrial settings along the bank of the Tyne northwards to rolling border wastes, Northumberland has a range of contrasting landscapes dotted with any number of striking landmarks and intriguing locations.

A handful of brick-built glass cones survive in Britain as a reminder of the eighteenth- and nineteenth-century glass-making industry. The oldest of these is located at Catcliffe, near Sheffield, but a later cone at Lemington, near Newcastle, is probably the largest brick cone in the world. Glass-making became a viable and important industry on Tyneside during the early years of the seventeenth century with supplies of cheap coal from local mines. By the mid-nineteenth century glass-making had become an important manufacturing industry and flint glass, crown glass for glazing and bottles were being produced. The Lemington works was opened in 1787 with the first glasshouse which was followed by three more.

The dramatic silhouette of a gallows stands close to the base of Steng Cross on open moorland near the village of Elsdon. In 1791 Margaret Crozier was found murdered at her home, Raw Peel, a little distance away to the north, and the evidence of a ten-year-old local lad named Richard Hindmarsh was instrumental in convicting William Winter of the crime. He had earlier seen Winter and two women accomplices at Whitlees Farm, Whiskerfield, and recognised a bootprint and unusual knife that were left at the scene of the crime. On 10 August 1792 the three were executed. The women's bodies were taken to the Surgeon's Hall at Newcastle for dissection while Winter's body was transported on a long cart to the highest point on Elsdon Moor. At this location it was hung from the gibbet for all to see and people travelled from miles around to view this ghoulish spectacle. Clothing and flesh rotted away until the body was wrapped in a tarred sack. Eventually the bones were scattered and the skull was taken away to Newcastle. A wooden head (or stob) was later hung from the chain and chips of wood from the original gibbet were at one time rubbed on the gums to cure toothache. The replacement structure stands on National Trust property as a gruesome reminder of these brutal events that left the young witness Richard Hindmarsh in fear of his life. After narrowly escaping death at his own home he spent time at Bywell before moving north of the border to the Aberdeen area. Before long he returned to Whiskerfield and died there in unknown circumstances at the young age of twenty-two.

A view of Lesbury.

Opposite, above: Lemington glass cone, probably the largest one in the world.

Opposite, below: Base of Steng Cross, near Elsdon.

The Old Mill, Lesbury.

Old Allendale in 1875.

Some place names have interesting or unusual connections. The tiny village of Blakehopeburnhaugh is noteworthy because it has the longest one-word name in the country (with eighteen letters). Cottonshopeburnfort has nineteen, but according to the spelling on Ordnance Survey maps it includes a hyphen (as do several other possible claimants). The straggling village of Lesbury is located at the highest tidal point on the River Aln where an imposing medieval two-arch bridge gives access to the nearby coastal settlement of Alnmouth. Lesbury's name originates from Laece Burg, the town of the leech or physician. Further north is the village of Lucker. Its name comes from Norse, meaning the 'marsh frequented by sandpipers' and this could be a reference to a peat bog at nearby Adderstone. Just over a century ago, during draining operations, a small oak box was recovered from about 6ft below the surface. Inside the box were twenty-two Roman copper coins, several horse harnesses and an apothecary's scale and beam. The coins dated from the reigns of Hadrian (AD 117–38) and Postumus (AD 260–7), with later ones in such good condition that it had been concluded that they had not long been in use. The whole collection was likely to have been hidden during a period of unrest following the usurpation of power by Postumus.

Allendale has several claims to fame. At the head of the valley, Allenhead is 1,400ft above sea level and is said to be England's highest village, while during the industrial boom period of the nineteenth century it had the most productive lead mine in the country. St Cuthbert's Church at Allendale town has a weathered sundial on its walls showing the town's latitude and longitude, in support of the township's claim to be at the centre of Britain (with the inclusion of the Channel Islands and Orkney). Recent debate has transferred this title to Haltwhistle, some 10 miles away to the north-west.

Some locations have links with earlier events. The scattered hamlet of Kyloe West lies just west of the A1 a few miles north of Belford and a group of nearby fir trees have the unusual name of Grizzy's Clump. In 1685 Grizel Cochrane, disguised as a man, held up the London mail coach at this spot and seized the death warrant of her brother, Sir John, who had been sentenced for his part in the Earl of Argyll's rebellion. Her intervention gave his friends time to obtain a pardon from King James II. Penny Hill, west of Woolsington Hall, takes its name from the days when horses were kept at the bottom of the incline and a charge of one penny was made for hiring a horse to haul heavy wagons to the top of the slope. Penny Pie Farm, north Blanchland, is a reminder of earlier times when travellers stopped at this remote farmstead for refreshment.

The delightful village of Harbottle lies among heather-covered hills at the upper end of Coquetdale (west of Rothbury). Ruined sections of the late twelfth-century castle look down on stone-built cottages, while the nearby Harbottle Crag is topped by the enormous Drake Stone. Slopes around the crag are jointly managed by Forest Enterprise and the Northumberland Wildlife Trust, and the range of wildlife to be found among scattered birch and rowan trees has led to the area's designation as a Site of Special Scientific Interest (SSSI). The

The path and bridge at Allendale in 1924.

underlying mass of fell sandstone was deposited some 300 million years ago, and down the centuries it has been quarried as building material by Roman invaders and, more recently, by John Dobson, designer of many buildings in Newcastle. Drake Stone stands among smaller boulders and measures 30ft in height, with an estimated weight of 2,030 tons. Along with nearby rocks, this massive boulder was broken off an adjacent crag and transported to its present location by an Ice Age glacier. A constant battering by the elements has eroded softer layers to expose cracks in its surface which have formed habitats for bilberry and heather. The origin of the name is unclear, but it has attracted an amount of folklore. At one time sick children were lifted over it to be cured, and when plans were made to drain nearby Harbottle Lough a mysterious voice is said to have issued the warning:

> Let alone, let alone
> Or I'll drown Harbottle
> And the Peels and the bonny Holystone.

Several locations in rural Northumberland are linked with the devil. The Devil's Lapful lies about a mile north of Bakethin Reservoir and is in fact a

Stone Age burial cairn, which is believed to date from around 2,800 BC. The association with the Devil stems from local folklore, which claims that he roamed around these parts with an apron full of stones. As he went on his way piles of rocks were deposited at intervals along his route, and an even larger heap, the Mutiny Stones, was dumped over the Scottish border above Dye Water in the Lammermuir Hills.

Dilston, near Corbridge, is said to derive its name Devil's Town from the Devil's Water which joins the Tyne close by. In reality the only buildings at this location are a mansion, a castle ruin and a disused church, for earlier glories were lost with the execution of the Earl of Derwentwater on 24 February 1716. He had taken a leading role in the Jacobite rising of the previous year, and was put to death on the scaffold at Tower Hill. On the night of his execution there was an exceptionally bright display of the Aurora Borealis which stained the Devil's Water a blood red colour and covered northern skies in glowing crimson. For years afterwards this spectacular natural episode was described as 'Lord Derwentwater's Lights'. The name Devil's Water may well originate from the Norman period when local lands were held by a baron with the surname D'Eivill.

Drake Stone.

Dilston Mill beside Devil's Water, near Corbridge.

Sir William Blackett of Wallington Hall is said to have served punch to guests at nearby Shaftoe Crags after his marriage in 1725.

The quiet little village of Doddington is located to the north of Wooler and may have developed around an ancient spring named the Dod Well, where water gushes from the foot of a basic stone cross. Standing about 20ft high, it was set up by the vicar in 1846. Away to the south lie the bracken-covered slopes of Dod Law, and on its south-facing aspect stands a 20ft high block of stone with vertical grooves. Local tradition claims that these marks were made by the chain when the Devil hanged his grandmother.

The summit of Shaftoe Crags is topped by a huge boulder with two deep circular hollows on its surface. Reports suggest that Sir William Blackett from Wallington Hall served punch to guests at this vantage point when he married in 1725.

The Devil's Causeway runs close to the A697 on its western side in the area near Longframlington and crosses the River Coquet near the village of Weldon. Whatever the origin of its name, the reality is that this route is a section of Roman roadway running northwards towards Tweedmouth.

Holy Island is renowned for dramatic events associated with the castle and priory, but another element of this location's intriguing history lay undiscovered for centuries. The village of Greenshiel, sited among sand dunes on the northern side of the island, was occupied during the ninth century before Viking raiders caused widespread destruction in 875. Evidence of the hamlet was uncovered during the nineteenth century when a wagon way was being laid to Kennedy Limeworks. In the mid-1980s archaeologists investigated the village site and their findings indicated that calves were reared here in order to provide skins which could be used to produce vellum, the material which formed the pages of the Lindisfarne Gospels.

Another location with an intriguing history spanning some 700 years is the expanse of Newcastle Town Moor. The territory was defined as common ground by King John in 1213 and the preservation of the moor since then has been described as unique in Britain. A total of around 1,000 acres of ground includes a sector of land between Grandstand Road and Claremont Road (349 acres), Nuns Moor, Castle Leazes, Hunters Moor, Dukes Moor and Little Moor. During 1996 an extensive archaeological survey revealed evidence of a prehistoric settlement, medieval and later ploughing patterns, traces of eighteenth- and nineteenth-century racecourses, aspects of the 1929 North East Coast Exhibition, Second World War defences and an Italian prisoner of war camp. The Castle Leazes area of the moor was first named in documents dating from 1357 when King Edward III re-affirmed rights to common law, and the Freemen of Newcastle are understood to have held grazing rights on the town's moor for many centuries before they were formalised in the 1774 Town Moor Act. In practice, freemen own the grass and the city council owns the soil with those grazing rights, ensuring that the Town Moor has remained as an integral and unaltered part of Newcastle's history.

The Cheviot Hills spread across some 300 square miles of the border between England and Scotland. They form a magnificent natural barrier and provide a range of habitats for bird, plant and insect life, while the slopes of the Cheviots are often the first landmark for vessels heading across the North Sea from Baltic ports. Those same valleys and slopes of the Cheviots and adjacent peaks have often been quoted as a graveyard for aircraft. During the Second World War Allied aircraft operated from several RAF stations in Northumberland, including Milfield, Acklington, Morpeth, Eshott, Woolsington and Ouston. In poor weather conditions aircrews would have difficulty navigating a course back to their home base. A memorial in the College Valley commemorates Allied airmen who lost their lives on the Cheviots during the war years. Enemy aircraft regularly plotted a course over the hills on the way to bomb Glasgow, and inevitably some did not return further than the border hills. During wartime local shepherds kept a watch for crashed aircraft, and in recent years they have often been first at the scene of light aircraft crashes.

9 Sports, Customs and Unusual Events

Northumberland's diverse border heritage is reflected not only in the range of outstanding buildings and extraordinary individuals but also through a host of remarkable customs, sporting occasions and unusual events.

Allendale town's wide main street, market place and solid stone houses have echoes of earlier lead mining days on adjacent moorland slopes. For much of the year the town attracts tourists and walkers to this southernmost sector of the county, but on New Year's Eve all the attention is focused on the annual custom that is played out in the market place. As midnight approaches twenty-four local men, known as guisers, make their way towards the centre of town. Dressed in a range of outrageous costumes including Viking helmets, Victorian miners' gear and fishnet tights, they balance flaming tar barrels on their heads as an accompanying brass band plays the Keel Row. Then, as the old year gives way to the new, a large bonfire is lit in the middle of the market place and the tar barrels are hurled into the flames in front of the King's Head Hotel. Sparks are scattered into the night sky as the band continues to provide musical support for dancing during this ceremony, which is said to be linked to ancient pagan beliefs where the old was burned off to allow the new to grow. For all the talk of age-old associations, it seems that this dramatic spectacle was first performed as recently as Queen Victoria's Diamond Jubilee (1897).

The tranquil atmosphere around the village of Elsdon remains undisturbed, but a closer look at the sloping green and surrounding area bears testimony to the status and importance of this remote location. A fourteenth-century pele tower has become the rectory and the splendid motte and bailey castle probably dates from about 1080, while early camps, cairns and earthworks are scattered around neighbouring hills. Since those days travellers between northern England and Scotland have used this route through Redesdale, but pagan practices continued at Elsdon well into the nineteenth century. Among the habits rooted in earlier heathen times was the driving of livestock through midsummer bonfires to stave off disease.

Alnwick's strategic position on high ground above the River Aln ensured its importance as a bastion against Scottish raiders along Northumberland's coastal strip. The town's castle has been the home of the Percy family since 1307 and this probably accounts for the air of antiquity and strength in the

Opposite, above: Allendale guisers on New Year's Eve in 1912.

Opposite, below: Tar-burning ceremony at Allendale on New Year's Eve.

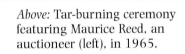

Above: Tar-burning ceremony featuring Maurice Reed, an auctioneer (left), in 1965.

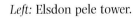

Left: Elsdon pele tower.

Hulne Priory with a statue of the praying monk.

The entrance to Hulne Priory (including photographer and camera).

Alnwick 'Dirty Bottles' in Ye Olde
Cross public house.

central buildings of the town. Parkland on the north-western side of the town is the setting for Hulne Priory, which was founded in about 1240 and shares with Aylesford in Kent the distinction of being the first English house of Carmelites or White Friars. Prominent among the remaining stonework is the Lord's Tower. It was constructed in about 1480 by the 4th Earl of Northumberland as a place of safety during Scottish raids and represents a rare example of a pele tower within a monastery. Closer to the town's northern edge is the site of Alnwick Abbey. A massive fourteenth-century gatehouse gave access to this base for Premonstratension Canons which was founded in 1147 by Eustace Fitz John. At one time the abbey possessed two valuable religious relics in the form of the chalice belonging to Thomas of Canterbury and a foot of Simon de Montfort fixed in a silver shoe. It was claimed that the foot was recovered from Royalist forces by de Montfort's supporters at the Battle of Evesham in 1265.

Below St Michael's Church lies a single row of estate houses for workers on the Duke of Northumberland's estates. Known as Canongate, this tiny sector of Alnwick at one time had its own mayor. Closer to the town centre, one of the many public houses, Ye Olde Cross, would seem at first impression to be linked with one of the nearby religious sites, but closer inspection reveals a

Alnwick castle gateway, starting point for the Shrove Tuesday football match.

Crowds on the Lion Bridge, at Alnwick, on their way to the playing field for the Shrove Tuesday football match.

rather different background. In fact, this humble hostelry is better known as the Dirty Bottles because of the collection of old glass bottles in a front window. Reports claim that an earlier licensee was arranging the display of glassware about 150 years ago when he was struck down by a sinister illness and died. Fears spread that anyone touching the bottles would also be affected by the fatal ailment, so the window recess was sealed up on the inside. The bottles have remained in the same place, slowly gathering a thick covering of dust and cobwebs, to this day.

A delightful stretch of riverside grassland runs eastwards from the Lion Bridge to the dramatic outlines of Denwick Bridge, where the parapet is created by interlacing crescents of the Percy Badge. These two splendid bridges served as the goals for the annual Shrove Tuesday football match, which was started from the castle gateway where a bewildering array of stone statues line the battlements. (They date from the eighteenth century and were carved by James Johnson of Stamfordham over some twenty years to imitate armed warriors fighting off an attack.) From this lofty location the ball was tossed down to participants who carried it out of town to the pastures where teams were organised. After the game the ball was lobbed into the river and whoever retrieved it was allowed to keep it.

Football matches have become part of local folklore in some areas. Border territory around Kielder is claimed to have been the setting for the first international football match between teams from England and Scotland. Soon after the union of the two countries under James in 1603, raiding parties from Liddesdale and Tindale allegedly called a halt to their incursions and arranged sporting contests to dissipate reserves of energy. Contemporary reports suggest that there were twenty players on each side with the game lasting until they were carried off the field in a state of exhaustion.

Horse racing enthusiasts in Northumberland flock to meetings at Newcastle and Hexham. Until about forty years ago there was another date on the racing calendar at a glorious natural setting to the west of Rothbury. Low ground on the south bank of the River Coquet first staged a meeting in April 1759 with races covering distances of between 2 and 3 miles. (The principal race, the Rothbury Cup, extended over 3 miles.) Racing was restricted to one meeting each year, always in April, apart from 1947 when the event was delayed until 31 May because the course was flooded. The years of 1915 to 1919 brought a temporary halt to Rothbury's race meetings, and racing did not restart after the Second World War until 1946. The final meeting was held on 10 April 1965, and since then the track has been adapted as a golf course with some of the former racecourse buildings now accommodating golf club premises.

During the late eighteenth century a popular leisure activity was to sample health-giving waters at fashionable spa locations such as Bath, Buxton or Harrogate. This craze even spread to the border country where spas were opened at some unlikely locations. The desolate wastes of Deadwater, to the north of

View of Haydon Spa at Haydon Bridge.

Kielder village, were singled out for the development of spa facilities during the late eighteenth century, and Armstrong's map of 1769 shows a bath and spa well. Situated quite close to the former Deadwater railway station, this remote setting was visited by people seeking cures for skin ailments. The coastal settlement of Spittal lies across the river from Berwick-upon-Tweed and probably derives its name from the thirteenth-century leper hospital that was dedicated to St Bartholomew. During the late eighteenth century the township attracted visitors from inland areas when spa waters were added to the list of seaside attractions. A number of villas were built to provide accommodation, including 31 High Street, which dates from 1792 and has a large walled garden at the rear. The original mineral spa well is located behind the war memorial on the southern side of the village and its waters were reported to be 'notable for curing the leprous and scorbutic humours of the blood'.

The healing properties of a spring at Bellingham were used to treat children suffering from rickets. According to local reports, the lady owner of Lee Hall used to immerse children in the waters before sunrise and then dip them in the River Tyne after sunset. At this point their clothes were thrown into the water, and if the bundle of clothes floated it was believed that the owner's rickets was cured.

A natural sulphur spring trickles from the hillside about a mile to the east of Haydon Bridge, but it took until 1863 before moves were made to develop the location. A group named the Haydon Bridge Picnic Committee received permission from the Receiver of the Greenwich Hospital Estates to clear the site and position a basin to collect the water. The local group added an inscribed stone above the basin and maintained access along the riverbank for a number of years, but by the end of the nineteenth century the path beside the Tyne had become partially blocked and landslips had covered the basin. During 1897 celebrations were held to mark Queen Victoria's Diamond Jubilee and the organising committee investigated a scheme to restore the spa well. Initial work was focused on cleaning the well and stone lintel before it was agreed that full restoration of the spa well would form a permanent memorial to the queen's jubilee. Social events and private donations raised around £100 as local people took a close interest in work at the spa site. Improvements to the footpath and walls around the spa were completed during May 1898 and on Whit Monday, 30 May 1898, the opening ceremony was performed by Mrs J.C. Straker. The Haydon Bridge Brass Band provided musical support as optimistic speeches and ambitious talk of weekend tickets for rail travellers prompted hopes of a new round of prosperity stemming from the spa. Such hopes did not materialise and the spa never acquired a hotel to serve visitors. In recent years sections of the path have collapsed and the well – within its brickwork and railings – remains inaccessible.

In some locations fragments of stone have been credited with special powers or qualities. At the east side of St Mary's churchyard on Holy Island is the bulky

Ladies' tug-of-war team at Bellingham gymkhana, 1920.

socket of St Cuthbert's Cross. Local tradition named it the Petting Stone, and if brides jumped over it then a happy marriage would follow. Heddon-on-the-Wall is best known for the 300yds long section of the Roman Wall, but below the township, on the north bank of the Tyne, a single stone was the focus for an unusual ceremony. Inscribed with the date 1785 and the coat of arms of Newcastle, it has marked the limit of the port's authority since at least 1292 and was known locally as the Kissing Stone. This term was linked with the ceremony of surveying the bounds (once every seven years) during which the Lord Mayor of Newcastle kissed a pretty girl at the stone. This setting also marked the highest tidal point on the Tyne until the river channel was widened and straightened.

The massive outlines of the Kielder Stone straddle the border between England and Scotland on the eastern slopes of Peel Fell. Standing some 26ft high and 46ft across, this huge mass of sandstone has been linked in local folklore with the Cout (Strong Man) of Kielder and sacrificial ceremonies. In more recent times the stone served as an unofficial post office, though an early belief persisted. It was considered unlucky to ride round it three times withershins – that is, the opposite way to the sun.

The raging waters of north country rivers presented problems for early bridge builders and many had to be rebuilt after serious floods. The splendid five-arched bridge over the North Tyne at Chollerford replaced an earlier structure that was built during the late fourteenth century on the orders of Bishop Skirlaw of Durham. A serious flood in 1771 had seriously damaged the earlier structure, and the present bridge was completed, with large cut-waters, some four years later. It has been suggested that Bishop Skirlaw's bridge may have been largely the work of convicts who were given a shorter sentence as a reward for their labour. As a result of this arrangement, it may have been known as The Gate to Heaven.

Coldstream Bridge spans the Tweed and consists of five impressive arches. It was designed by John Smeaton and constructed between 1763 and 1766 with a row of false flood openings above the main buttresses. An unusual feature at the north side of the bridge is a red-tiled marriage house where runaway couples could become man and wife with very little ceremony. One local yarn recalls an incident when a would-be bridegroom shot the horse of his pursuer at Cornhill in order to gain enough breathing space for a hasty marriage across the river. These rapidly arranged marriages were stopped in 1856 and eloping couples had to make the longer journey to Gretna Green.

During the mid-seventeenth century authorities in Newcastle had rather strange methods of dealing with offenders. A common drunkard was led through the streets as a subject of derision by being covered by a large barrel, known as a Newcastle Cloak. One side had holes for his hands with another opening in the top for his head. Scolds wore an iron headpiece called the branks that was shaped like a crown. It spread down to the neck and included a tongue of iron which reached into the mouth and subdued the most argumentative of individuals.

10 Those Daring, Dashing, Devilish Delavals

Through the generations most noble families have produced a cluster of flamboyant and extravagant individuals, but few, if any, can equal the outrageous antics of the Delaval family. More often than not there are few details about the indiscretions, vices and wrong-doings of aristocratic family members, but in the case of the Delavals a whole collection of personal documents give us a fascinating and detailed insight into their astonishing lifestyle.

The Delaval family can trace their origins back to Hubert de la Val, a cousin of William of Normandy, who was rewarded for his support at the Battle of Senlac Hill (Hastings) in 1066 with a tract of land in mid-Northumberland. Successive members of the family held public office in their home area and were involved in border warfare with the Scots. The first mention of a family house appears in 1415 – with reference to a tower that was probably located close to the present Seaton Delaval Hall. By 1549 a beacon on the top of the tower was one of a series that would be lit to give warning of impending invasion. During the late 1620s the buildings were extended, and there is a hint of events to come as Sir Ralph Delaval entertained large numbers of guests in grand style. Following his death the family's wealth was squandered and it was his grandson, another Sir Ralph, who retrieved the situation by developing facilities for salt and coal shipments at nearby Seaton Sluice.

On his death there was further uncertainty about the Delaval family inheritance before it passed in 1717 to a distant cousin and sea-going man, Captain (later Admiral) George Delaval. He was determined to use much of his accumulated wealth to replace the decaying medieval manor house with a more impressive family home, so he began by planting the avenue of trees on the approach to the hall. Admiral George commissioned Sir John Vanburgh to design the new family seat, but before work was completed the admiral was fatally injured in a fall from his horse.

The Seaton Delaval estate now passed to George's nephew, Francis Delaval, a Royal Navy captain, who had already acceded to Ford Castle on his mother's death. A condition of the inheritance was that if he was bequeathed Seaton Delaval then the Ford estate would be handed over to his mother's sister, but with

Approach to Seaton Delaval Hall from the north.

Seaton Delaval Hall, south front.

complete disregard for this arrangement, the Delaval crest of a Ram's Head was installed above the door at Ford. Local legend suggests that sometime later the ram's head was heard to state that as long as the Ford estate was linked with Seaton Delaval, no male member of the family would die in his bed. Coincidence or otherwise, the reality remains that neither Captain Delaval, nor seven of his eight sons, nor his grandson died in bed. The other son, Edward, died peacefully in his bed at the age of eighty-five after Ford Castle had been handed over to his great niece, Susanna, Marchioness of Waterford.

Seaton Delaval Hall was completed, to Vanburgh's designs, in 1729 at a cost to Captain Francis Delaval of £10,000, but marriage to a wealthy heiress from Huntingdonshire, Rhoda Apreece, ensured his future financial security. He abandoned his naval career and fathered eleven children before the family curse struck. On 9 December 1752 Captain Delaval tripped and fell down the steps of the south front portico, broke his leg and died soon afterwards.

Family wealth passed to the eldest son, Francis, a debonair twenty-five year old newly elected member of parliament for Hindon, who passed his time entertaining his mistress and staging amateur theatricals at London venues.

On one notable occasion Francis hired the Theatre Royal, Drury Lane, in order to stage a family production of *Othello*. An audience of royalty, noble families and members of parliament headed to the venue, with the House of Commons reportedly adjourning two hours early to allow their attendance.

Seaton Delaval Hall, north frontage.

The cost of staging the event at Francis's expense came to £1,500 and he duly starred as Othello with his brothers John and Thomas playing the parts of Iago and Cassio. Emilio was played by Elizabeth Roach, who was Francis Delaval's mistress. By all accounts the standard of acting left much to be desired, but the fact that the cast was composed of the infamous Delaval family and their associates drew capacity audiences.

When they were not occupied in staging dramatic productions, Francis Delaval and his cronies set up business as fortune tellers and miracle workers. Using any number of disguises and devious trickery, they fleeced gullible rich clients, such as Lady Isabella Paulet, out of large sums of money. She was persuaded to marry Francis and brought with her a dowry of £23,000, which was rapidly squandered by her husband on gifts for his mistress, Elizabeth Roach. The marriage lasted five years and soon afterwards Lady Isabella died.

Francis Delaval's outrageous lifestyle necessitated the services of a lawyer, William Kelynge, who regularly risked life and limb when supporting his client. Francis was knighted in 1760 and during the following year he contested a parliamentary seat at Andover. Using cash raised by the sale of precious family silver from Seaton Delaval, he rewarded local voters for their support and decided

Seaton Delaval Hall, west wing.

The interior of Seaton Delaval Hall.

to hold a celebratory banquet at the George Inn. With more than a touch of Sir Francis's trickery, Kelynge sent out invitations to army officers as if from the mayor and to the mayor as if from army officers. Each group believed that the other was paying for the banquet and the unfortunate William Kelynge was still in the room when they became aware of his double dealing. His subsequent bill to Sir Francis reached £500, and included the surgeon's fees for tending his broken leg and loss of time from work.

During a previous general election campaign at Andover, Francis had canvassed support by firing 500 golden guineas from a cannon and won over an arch opponent by arranging a fire-eating display by one of his cronies. However, by 1758 he was seeking fresh adventures and after joining the army Francis led a landing party of grenadiers on to the beach of St Malo in Brittany. The assault was unopposed, but his backers made the most of the incident in the successful bid to gain a knighthood (which succeeded in 1760).

When he was not pursuing his hectic lifestyle of riotous pleasure in London and the south of England, Francis and his entourage converged on family members at Doddington in Lincolnshire or at Seaton Delaval, where his sister lived in the west wing of the hall. Feasting and practical jokes were the order of the day with sack races and rope dancing followed by banquets for up to 4,000 guests. When visitors eventually retired to bed they faced the prospect of sleeping in beds that collapsed unexpectedly or gently sank into a cold bath in the middle of the night. If Francis and his supporters tired of the practical jokes then there were always wagers to be laid. During one gathering at Seaton Delaval, he boasted that he could walk blindfold in a straight line from the pleasure gardens to the steps on the South Front. A fine silk thread was stretched out to guide him across the lawns, but unbeknown to Francis the trail had been seen and was then rerouted across one of the lily ponds. He may have lost that particular wager in a particularly embarrassing manner but on another occasion he was spectacularly successful. The circumstances are not clear, but it seems that he was challenged to build a castle over just one night and bets were laid. Sir Francis had prepared sections of a small tower in advance and sure enough the castle was assembled during the hours of darkness. He won his wager and portions of Starlight Castle still crown a small hillock overlooking the Seaton Burn.

Apart from his visits to relatives at Dissington and Seaton Delaval, Francis spent much of his time in London where he fathered two children, Frank and Fanny, with Elizabeth Roach before she left him in 1758. He soon came across another lady companion, but Ann Catley's father successfully sued him in court for conspiracy to debauch his daughter and Francis was left to pay a fine and costs amid a hail of mockery.

While Francis Delaval was frittering away family riches in the capital, his brothers and sisters were putting their wealth to good use in northern locations. During 1768 Seaton Sluice was at the peak of its industrial output with coal shipments, brickworks and bottle factory working at full capacity. A New Cut,

Seaton Delaval Hall from the south-west.

The Cut at Seaton Sluice.

The Mausoleum, Seaton Delaval Hall.

constructed between 1761 and 1764 gave direct access to the sea via a channel blasted through solid rock with gates that could be opened and closed with tides. In 1768 Sir Francis did provide an enduring contribution to the Seaton Delaval estate in the form of a grand stable, but it was expenditure he could not afford. During the following year he borrowed £10,000 from his brother-in-law, Lord Mexborough, but within twelve months he had squandered it and was forced to move in with his relatives. Lonely and desolate, Sir Francis died on 7 August 1771 at the age of forty-four. His few earthly possessions amounted to one carriage, five horses and his underwear and the costs associated with his funeral amounted to £690. Following a three-week journey from London to Seaton Delaval, via Newcastle, he was buried in the Church of Our Lady close to the hall.

Francis Delaval left no legitimate heirs and his brother, John, moved to Seaton Delaval from Doddington as the industrial enterprises prospered. However, the closing years of the eighteenth century marked the peak of the family's fortunes. John Delaval was assisted by his brother, Thomas, but the curse that afflicted this amazing family struck again in 1787 when Thomas was fatally injured in a fall from his horse during an outing in Hyde Park, London.

Sir John's Delaval's family troubles were unrelenting. His only son, Jack, had died in 1775 at the age of twenty 'as a result of having been kicked in a vital organ by a laundry maid to whom he was paying his addresses' and by the time Sir John became a peer in 1783 both his wife Susanna and daughter Elizabeth had also died. In an attempt, perhaps, to lift his spirits, Lord John Delaval revived theatrical events at Seaton Delaval Hall, and the Christmas seasons of 1790 and 1791 featured four productions including *Othello* and a contemporary play called *The Fair Penitent*. Cast members included not only Lord Delaval but also other family members such as his daughter Sarah, Lady Tyrconnel, her husband and her lover.

At the age of seventy John Delaval brought a young woman, Elizabeth Hicks, to the household at Seaton Delaval, but after little more than a year she died at the tender age of twenty-three. Her place on the domestic scene was taken by another young woman, Susanna Knight, and in 1803, at the age of seventy-five, Lord Delaval married her at the parish church at Earsdon. The marriage lasted for five years until the Delaval curse struck again when John Delaval collapsed and died at the breakfast table in May 1808.

The terms of Lord Delaval's will divided the estates of Ford and Seaton Delaval. Ford Castle passed to his granddaughter, Susanna, Marchioness of Waterford, while his brother, Edward, took over at Seaton Delaval. When Edward died, in

St Mary's Church, Seaton Delaval.

bed, in 1814 the curse on the Delavals was broken, but a final drama was yet to be played out. In January 1822 a massively destructive fire swept through Seaton Delaval Hall. Although the central block was completed gutted, the east and west wings were saved and family papers that provide such a close insight into their lavish lifestyle were rescued.

Following Edward's death there were no legitimate male Delavals to receive the inheritance and the hall passed to the Astley family from Norfolk. For more than a century the main block remained as a gutted shell after plans from John Dobson proved too costly in the 1860s and it was Sir Edward Delaval Henry Astley, 22nd Baron Hastings, who undertook a programme of restoration. In 1950 he re-roofed the east and west wings and started to clear debris from the main block, and between 1959 and 1963 further extensive repairs were carried out. The old kitchens were brought back into use for staging medieval banquets and other areas were opened for public viewing during summer months. Today Vanburgh's architectural masterpiece looks out proudly across the mid-Northumberland landscape with the tiny church of St Mary close at hand on the western side. Modern housing developments have edged towards the hall on the southern boundary and the industrial setting has changed considerably at nearby Seaton Sluice since ships passed through the New Cut close to the curious Octagon House that probably served as the harbour master's quarters. Close by, overlooking the Seaton Burn, Starlight Castle provides a hint of the Delaval's frivolous lifestyle, but the true spirit of this outrageous family really comes to life in the great hall where the charred columns and statues seem to echo the sounds of merry-making, theatrical productions and practical jokes.

11 Berwick-upon-Tweed: The Land in Between

There is an air of independent defiance around the streets, walls and riverside of England's most northerly town, Berwick-upon-Tweed. In fact this border town was at one time separate from both Scotland and England and as the County of the Borough and Town of Berwick-upon-Tweed it had to be given special mention in Acts of Parliament until 1746. Over the centuries Berwick is said to have withstood more sieges than any other town except Jerusalem, and during the border wars Berwick changed hands thirteen times before finally being attached to the English crown.

During the turbulent medieval period towns were often encircled by fortified walls to deter invaders. In addition to the dramatic fortifications that encircle York there are other fragmentary examples in the north country at Hartlepool and Newcastle upon Tyne, as well as the Hotspur Gate that formed part of Alnwick's town walls. Berwick's medieval walls covered some 2 miles in length and were constructed during the reign of Edward II (1284–1327), but little of this structure remains intact. The impressive fortifications that encompass the centre of Berwick date from the 1550s when fears of a Franco-Scottish invasion were high. Their design is based on similar schemes at Lucca, Verona and Antwerp where two Italian engineers Contio and Portinari were in charge of building work, but the main designer at Berwick was an Englishman, Sir Richard Lee. Unique in Britain, they are probably the best-surviving example of their kind in Europe and achieve an efficient beauty of line along with forbidding strength. Massive sloping walls some 12ft thick at the base were backed by a huge bank of earth to deflect cannonballs and withstand sustained artillery fire. At each corner there was an enormous bastion (of which Mag's Mount, Brass Bastion, Cumberland Bastion and Windmill Bastion are the best examples), and from these positions flanking fire could be directed across every possible line of approach to the walls. It is perhaps not surprising that the only wartime damage sustained by these impregnable defences resulted from target practice by home-based bren gunners.

Stonework from Berwick's old castle was used to construct the Royal Border Bridge, the barracks and the parish church of Holy Trinity. Apart from the chancel, which was added in 1855, the building dates from the late 1640s and

Berwick-upon-Tweed town walls.

Holy Trinity Church, Berwick-upon-Tweed.

is one of only two churches in Britain dating from the Commonwealth period. The architect was John Young, Master of the Masons Company, and it is said that plans for a tower were dropped at Oliver Cromwell's insistence. Among the many monuments within the church, there is a decorative tablet on the south wall commemorating Colonel George Fenwick who died in 1656. He was governor of Berwick and a close associate of Cromwell. An inscription states that he was 'a principal instrument of causing this church to be built. A good man is a public good'. During the mid-seventeenth century English architecture was experiencing one of its great periods of change. The ascendancy of the Gothic style was giving way to domination by the classical, and Holy Trinity stands at the centre of the change, successfully embodying ideas from both styles.

A faded gravestone in Holy Trinity churchyard showing skull and crossbones is believed to mark the burial place of a plague victim during an outbreak in the summer of 1665. Ships taking coal to London from north-east ports brought the plague to Sunderland, Gateshead and Newcastle, but Berwick's mayor was warned by letter about the plague and put in place measures to prevent an outbreak. Ships, sailors and cargoes were quarantined on the River Tweed for six weeks, barrels were cleaned and guards at the town gates turned away travellers without a certificate of health. These measures seem to have prevented a large-scale outbreak of the plague, as the parish records for 1665–6 show no increase in the number of burials compared with earlier years.

Another indication of Berwick's importance as a frontier town is provided by the barracks. Dating from 1719, they were designed either by Sir John Vanburgh or by Andrew Jelf, architect to the Ordnance Department, with guidance from the master architect, and represent the earliest barrack building in Britain.

The soaring spire of Berwick's town hall occupies a central position at the lower end of the main thoroughfare, Marygate. It was designed by Samuel Worrall, Master of the London Masons Company and constructed during the late 1750s by Joseph Dodds (whose name appears above the main entrance). A graceful lantern and spire soar 150ft above the central portico with housing for eight bells, one of which was rung as a curfew at eight every weekday evening. Four of the bells belong to Holy Trinity Church, as it has no tower, and are rung for Sunday services.

Wallace Green, an open area between the barracks and the sea, is the setting for a procession known as Riding the Bounds. It has traditionally taken place on 1 May each year and covers almost 8 miles of outlying routes. It originated after the boundary of Berwick had been defined by treaty with the Scots in 1438.

The River Tweed has played a major role in Berwick's development as a border town, with high ground offering a defensive location to guard crossing points and as a link between the hinterland and sea-going vessels using riverside facilities. The oldest of the town's three bridges was constructed from red sandstone between 1610 and 1634 with the King's Surveyor at Berwick, James Burrell, directing operations. Its fifteen arches vary in height and width as they spread

Town hall, Berwick-upon-Tweed.

The Old Bridge at Berwick-upon-Tweed.

across the waters of the Tweed, prompting one uncharitable critic to liken them to a herd of elephants crossing the river. Most observers would probably agree that the bridge's diverse dimensions have a certain charm and, without doubt, it represents a fine contrast with the adjacent Royal Border Bridge (1847–50) and the New Bridge (1925–8).

The waters of the Tweed also provide a rich harvest for salmon fishermen (during the season from mid-February to mid-September). Some use a flat-bottomed boat, known as a cobble, to catch fish. Two men hold one end of the net in the cobble while a third holds the other end on the shore. The net is drawn out to its full length before four more men help to haul in the catch, which can amount to fifty salmon.

Some aspects of Berwick's fascinating past are less obvious. The fishing industry was a major factor in the town's continued prosperity and ice was first used to preserve salmon at Berwick in 1788. Before long it had replaced boiling, smoking, salting and curing as the preferred means of preserving fish for markets in London and the south. As demand for ice increased rapidly three ice houses were built in Berwick during the 1790s, and in 1799 a total of 7,600 cartloads of ice were gathered. An interesting example of one of Berwick's ice houses is

Wellington Terrace, Berwick-upon-Tweed.

The old town, Berwick-upon-Tweed.

to be found at Bank Hill. A report in 1799 stated that 'the aspect of icehouses should be towards the east or south east for the advantage of the morning sun to expel the damp air, as that is more precious than warmth for which reason trees in the vicinity of an ice house tend to its disadvantage'. During the nineteenth century, the Tweed salmon trade required huge amounts of ice and most was provided from local sources such as Heatherytops Farm, near Scremerston and, during severe winters, from the river itself. Extensive icehouses were constructed below the Customs House, and in Shoregate and throughout the town icehouses had a capacity for storing a total of 1,600 tons of ice. A workforce of about thirty men was needed to pack the ice into chambers within the average commercial icehouse. During the 1860s manufactured ice began to go on sale in Britain. This development signalled the beginning of the end for commercial icehouses, but it was not until 1951 that the Salmon Company set up an ice-making plant at its riverside base. More than half a century later – in the early twenty-first – the icehouse at Bank Hill has found an alternative use as a builder's store, while other examples of these fascinating industrial chambers lie unnoticed beneath the streets of Berwick.

Perhaps it was the abundance of salmon in the nearby river that influenced William Wilson's design work on the frontage of 48 Tweed Street, Berwick. Each stone has been etched with an abstract pattern that has an overall appearance of fish scales, while all the windows are crowned with a carved head. The actual

Quay Walls, Berwick-upon-Tweed.

reason for this wealth of decorative detail remains unknown, but William Wilson repeated the exercise on an even larger scale at 178 Main Street, Spittal (across the river from Berwick). Maybe we should only conclude that he was fulfilling a flight of fishy fantasy.

Berwick-upon-Tweed's border setting has generated any number of curious outcomes. In geographical terms the town is part of the county of Northumberland, yet the local population seem to speak with an accent that is more Scottish than Northumbrian, and in common with other Scottish border towns like Moffatt, Jedburgh and Hawick, Berwick has its own special item of confectionery, the Berwick Cockle. A glance along Quay Walls with the impressive Custom House shows some splendid architectural details such as sash windows with unusual horizontal panes that are quite commonplace in Scotland but rarely found further south in England. Perhaps strangest of all from this land in between was the rumour that Berwick had been at war with Russia since the Crimean War. The rumour persisted from 1914 to 1965 and originated from the town's diplomatic peculiarity which necessitated separate Acts of Parliament up to 1746. Even after that time royal proclamations and state documents occasionally gave Berwick the distinction of a separate mention. It is suggested that when Queen Victoria signed the declaration of war with Russia on 28 March 1854 she used the title Victoria, Queen of Great Britain, Ireland, Berwick upon Tweed and the British Dominions beyond the seas. When peace was negotiated in 1856 there was no mention of the border town and the rumour persisted that Berwick had declared war but not concluded peace. Stories along these lines circulated in 1914 and again in 1935 when the *Daily Telegraph* focused attention on the apparent ongoing hostilities between England's border town and the might of Russia. The rumour was finally laid to rest in 1965 when town officials took up the matter with the Foreign Office. They investigated the situation and found no supporting evidence for the claims, but this curious episode certainly added weight to Berwick's anomalous position as a buffer town between England and Scotland.

12 A Legacy of Roman Riddles

From legal code to civil engineering projects, the conquering Roman legions left an amazing legacy for future generations in their northern province of Britain. A most dramatic reminder of the Roman presence is Hadrian's Wall, which takes the name of the emperor who prompted its construction in about AD 122. At other times it has also been called the Roman Wall or the Picts' Wall after the tribes it was supposed to have been built to hold at bay. In fact the wall represents only one component of the defences that made up the Roman frontier. Running along the north side of the wall, apart from stretches where the ground was steep, ran a wide ditch. Every mile along it was a milecastle or fort and between milecastles there were turrets. At key locations there were forts to house garrisons of troops and along the south side of the wall ran a flat-bottomed ditch with an earth bank on each side called a vallum. Linked with the 73-mile long main section of the wall were milecastles and turrets stretching along the west coast, outpost forts to the north of the wall and the Roman port on the Tyne at South Shields (Arbeia).

Construction of the wall was completed almost totally by troops from three Roman legions: the 20th based at Chester, the 6th from York and the 2nd which was stationed at Caerleon in South Wales. There is no evidence to indicate use of a large local labour force, and it seems that the legions contained all the specialist craftsmen needed to complete the building work, although locals were probably used for the most basic tasks.

Completion of this massive structure must have made a considerable impact on the lives of local people and archaeological research has thrown up some fascinating speculative theories. At a location known as Milking Gap, just west of Housesteads, archaeologists uncovered a farmstead, which was deserted at around the time of the wall's construction, possibly because it was located inside the new military zone. Farming activities would have been affected by the line of the wall and it is believed that the Knag Burn gate at Housesteads may have been inserted into the structure during the fourth century to allow movement of livestock from one side of the wall to the other. Completion of the wall also brought a much larger number of soldiers to this northern sector of Britain, and such a build up inevitably increased the demand for locally grown food. In all probability, this need for more cereals would have resulted in changes to local farming methods, but so far there is only limited archaeological evidence to support this theory.

THE ROMAN WALL

THE ROAD OF THE ROMAN
TOUR BY RAIL OR ROAD

Cawfields milecastle on Hadrian's Wall.

Apart from the economic effects on the immediate locality, construction of the wall undoubtedly resulted in changes on the social scene as growing civilian settlements attracted merchants, farmers and soldiers' families. Roman soldiers were not officially permitted to marry until they had served their time in the army, but there was nothing to prevent them from contracting agreements with women according to local law. When a soldier retired this arrangement would be recognised in Roman law. Few personally dedicated tombstones have been discovered, but one example was uncovered at Petriana (Stanwix) north of Carlisle with an inscription from a widow to her deceased soldier husband: 'To the Divine Shades of Marcus Troianius Augustinus; his dearest wife Aelia Ammillusima, saw the making [of this tomb].'

A number of remarkable discoveries were made at the civilian centre of Vindolanda, south of Housesteads, during 1973. The number of wooden writing tablets that were unearthed represented a much larger quantity than previously found on a Roman British site. Soil conditions at Vindolanda ensured that writing, on both sides of the tablets, was in a remarkable state of preservation. The writing was in pen and ink, with perhaps the most intriguing extract referring to

Opposite: LNER poster advertising the Roman wall, 1925.

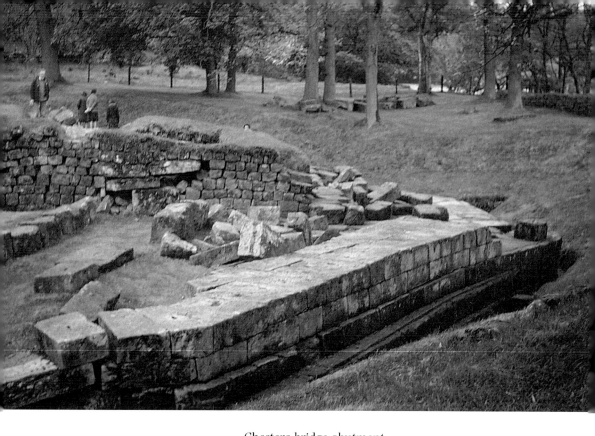

Chesters bridge abutment.

Bathhouse from the bridge abutment at Chesters.

An aerial view of Housesteads fort, Hadrian's Wall.

the sending of two pairs of sandals, an unknown number of woollen socks and two pairs of underpants. Roman soldiers were responsible for their own clothing and a deduction was made from their pay to cover such costs, so the unknown recipient of the goods would no doubt have been extremely grateful.

A Roman mile corresponds to approximately 1,620yds and consisted of 'milia passum' (a thousand paces), but for all their road building, examples of Roman milestones are hard to find. The only Roman milestone in England that is still located in its original position is set beside Stanegate, near Vindolanda, and measures 6ft in height.

Sewingshields milecastle lies about 2 miles east of Housesteads fort and is one of many places on the wall that are linked with legends of King Arthur. Tradition maintains that King Arthur and his court lay in a hypnotic sleep in a cave or hall below a castle. The spell would only be broken when someone found a way to the cave, blew a bugle and cut a garter with the 'sword of the stone'. A local farmer is supposed to have found the hidden cave and cut the garter, but forgot to blow the bugle first. King Arthur and his knights stirred from their sleep but the spell was improperly broken and they soon sank back into their slumbers.

Another legend is connected with the King's Crag and the Queen's Crag, two oddly shaped sandstone outcrops that stand about half a mile apart in front of the Roman wall. Arthur was said to have perched on one crag before hurling a

Milecastle at Gilsland.

20-ton boulder towards Guinevere who was combing her hair on the other crag. She managed to deflect the giant stone that now rests between the crags and it clearly shows marks from her comb – so the story runs.

A box of treasure is said to lie in the depths of nearby Broomlee Lough and at the bottom of the cliff face it is possible to follow the line of a baffling earthwork, called the Black Dyke, that runs northwards across open moorland. It has been followed from Moralee on the South Tyne through to Tarset on the North Tyne and may well have formed a pre-Norman boundary mark.

Housesteads fort covers some 5 acres and represents the best-known location along the length of Hadrian's Wall. Around the fort was a thriving community and a part of this settlement can be identified outside the south gate of the military base. Facing on to the southern roadway through the township is a building that became known as Murder House. Behind a shop frontage was a large living room and during excavations in 1932 researchers uncovered evidence of a Roman crime. Beneath a fresh clay floor were the skeletons of a middle-aged man and woman, and the discovery of a broken sword point in the man's ribs pointed to murder. Roman law specifically prohibited burial within a civilian settlement and the care taken to conceal the bodies leaves little doubt about the nature and seriousness of the crime. The property is believed to have been completed in about AD 300 and deserted in 367, so the murders must have been

A view of excavations at Corstopitum (Corbridge).

The Corbridge Lion, which was a fountain head, is regarded as one of the finest pieces of Celtic Roman sculpture to have been uncovered in Britain.

carried out between these dates, but the motive for the crime and identities of those involved will remain unknown.

Corbridge was built at a strategically important location where Stanegate (running westwards to Carlisle) crossed Dere Street (which linked Scotland with London and the south). At the heart of the township stood an impressive fountain and a series of temples with fine ornamental stonework. It was occupied until the withdrawal of Roman forces during the early fifth century, and Corbridge was one of the first Roman sites to be investigated when treasure seekers arrived here in the reign of King John. One of the most dramatic items of stonework is the Corbridge Lion, which stood on a fountain of a house to the south of the military areas. It features a gluttonous lion, measuring about 2ft 6in in length, standing on the back of a lamb and may well have been designed for part of a tomb.

Over the centuries much of the stonework from Hadrian's Wall has been removed and reused in other buildings. Some of the most intriguing examples of re-worked Roman masonry are to be seen in the former school building at Rochester (north-west of Otterburn on the A68). The property is now a private house, and in the porch it is possible to pick out stones that were used to construct the nearby fort of Bremenium. Some of the stones had clearly been hollowed out to form a gutter. Two round stones in the gable of the house probably weigh about 1cwt. It has been suggested that they were ammunition fired from a Roman ballista. Whether they were actually fired in anger or came from an ammunition dump remains open to speculation. Other sections of stonework from the Roman fort are still to be seen on the village green.

Metal detecting enthusiasts at Morpeth made an intriguing discovery in February 2003. A total of about seventy coins made from valueless bronze were uncovered, and experts believe that resourceful local townsfolk were in the business of melting down Roman coins and turning the metal into trinkets such as necklaces and brooches. The bronze items were traded with occupying Roman soldiers. Earlier archaeological research had proved that the Romans recycled metal, but until this discovery there was no evidence that local inhabitants did this. It also indicated that there was a relationship between native and military populations.

13 Vanished Glories

A review of the past clearly illustrates the transient nature of power and influence among nations as successive empires have achieved positions of dominance – only to decline and fade over subsequent years. The same phenomenon applies to some rural communities, where today's tranquil settings offer clues to earlier greatness.

The village of Kirknewton is surrounded by hills, and little more than half a mile away to the south-east lie the impressive outlines of Yeavering Bell. Standing some 1,182ft high, its spreading summit and slopes were an important location for early settlers. Over 4,000 years ago Stone Age people lined up a sacred monument to face this impressive landmark and around 500 BC an Iron Age hill fort was constructed over some 15 acres of the highest level. A total of about 130 round houses were protected by an immense stone rampart that encloses one of the largest Iron Age settlements in Northern Britain.

Some 1,100 years later, in about AD 600, Anglo Saxon settlers built a royal village at Gefrin just north of Yeavering Bell. It is thought to be the seventh-century timber palace of Edwin of Northumbria referred to in the writings of the Venerable Bede. Generally, when Anglo-Saxons occupied significant Ancient British sites they renamed them, and in this case they adopted the local name Gefrin. Down the years this has become the current Yeavering, which means, 'the hill of the goats'.

At Old Yeavering on the northern slopes of Yeavering Bell a low farm building has walls that are 5ft thick, which may have formed a section of a pele tower. It probably dates from the early sixteenth century and would have offered protection during the time of border reivers, but local folklore linked this sturdy structure with Gefrin and it became known as the Old Palace. This impressive location poses more questions than answers and, though many of its secrets may never be fully explained, there is no doubt that Yeavering Bell has been a location of considerable status and importance for around 4,000 years.

A scattering of properties at Bolam, a few miles south-west of Morpeth, give little indication of this setting's earlier importance. During the medieval period Bolam was a large medieval township, which was granted a market by Royal Charter in 1305. Bolam House stands on the site of a medieval castle within the outlines of an early British encampment where traces of the bank and ditches can be identified. Adjacent parkland with a lake, wooded island and reed beds was designed by John Dobson in 1818.

Gefrin, near Kirknewton.

On the south side of the village Shortflatt Tower is a fine example of a fourteenth-century pele tower (with later extensions to form comfortable domestic quarters), and close at hand on the west side stands Harnham Hall. Remains of an early castle are located behind the modern residence, and in the garden is a cave where Katherine Babington was buried in 1670. She was the daughter of Sir Arthur Hesilrige, an important parliamentary leader during the English Civil War, and wife of Major Babington, Governor of Berwick. Her unusual burial place resulted from an incident when she was found guilty of bribing a butcher boy to drag a parson from the pulpit. This resulted in her excommunication and interment in the cave, but some years later a band of gypsies plundered the rocky tomb and her bones were scattered on nearby ground.

St Andrew's Church at Bolam once overlooked a township of around 200 houses. Its tall west tower dates from the late Saxon period, but most of the remainder of the building was completed by Norman craftsmen. The south chapel has two intriguing features – one ancient and the other modern. A huge trefoiled niche in the east wall has hinges for double doors and, by contrast, a little window with plain glass is set in beautiful contemporary lead work. An inscription gives details of an amazing wartime episode when four bombs were dropped by German aircraft on 1 May 1942. Three exploded outside the church and the fourth travelled into the building through an old doorway. Its mechanism had been torn away as it passed among trees in the churchyard and it came to rest inside the chapel without exploding.

Bywell is set in glorious natural surroundings overlooking the Tyne about 12 miles west of Newcastle. A handful of properties, two old churches and a dignified stone mansion provide few indications of the size and importance of the township during the medieval period. Construction of a bridge gave Bywell increased eminence under the Baliol family of Barnard Castle, but after the crown seized the lands in 1294 Bywell had several owners before it passed to the Nevilles in 1376. They retained possession until the religious troubles of 1569 and were responsible for construction of the castle with battlements and corner turrets in about 1430 – probably under Ralph Neville. The location of the castle is unusual, as it was not positioned on high ground or overlooking the bridge but at the end of the village where a high-walled enclosure offered protection for villagers and their livestock. Henry VI is reported to have found refuge here after fleeing from the battlefield at Hexham on 8 May 1464.

Bywell's prosperity stemmed from iron-making, with craftsmen fashioning bits, stirrups, buckles and other items for horsemen and noble households. Nearby

The market cross at Bywell.

St Andrew's Church, Bywell.

woodland provided fuel for the industrial processes as well as red deer and game for food, while the closeness of the Tyne ensured a plentiful supply of salmon. In 1570 there were fifteen shops in the settlement ranged along one long street between the castle and the two churches. By the mid-nineteenth century the last shop had disappeared, and at about the same time the thirteenth-century village cross was repositioned in a field near the hall.

Bywell Hall was designed by James Paine and completed in about 1760 for the Fenwick family. It included sections of an older property, which was altered and extended by John Dobson during 1817.

Another curious feature at Bywell is the two parish churches, St Andrew's and St Peter's, which stand in close proximity. One local tale suggests that wealthy sisters who quarrelled and tried to out-rival each other built the two churches. Another story describes them as the Black Church (St Peter's through its links with black-robed Benedictine monks from Durham) and the White Church (of St Andrew because of the association with white-robed Premonstratensian clerics from Blanchland). In fact, both buildings are parish churches that date from earlier days when Bywell was divided into two separate parishes. St Andrew's has a splendid west tower with a lower section dating from the ninth century and an upper portion dating from about 1000. A pillar within the church supports part of the shaft from a Saxon cross and the plain octagonal font probably dates from the thirteenth century. St Andrew's also has an amazing collection of medieval cross-slab grave covers. Eighteen of the twenty-five items were re-set in the outside face of the north wall and others have been used as lintels over internal doorways and windows. St Andrew's was declared redundant in 1973 and taken into the care of the Churches Conservation Trust two years later.

Parts of the northern side of St Peter's Church are Anglo-Saxon and date from the 790s whereas the short tower is built on Norman foundations. The north chapel was built as a chantry in the mid-fourteenth century and until the 1850s it served as a school, while the south arcade and eastern section of the chancel date from the thirteenth century. St Peter's churchyard was damaged by floods on Sunday 17 November 1771 when rising waters swept away coffins and destroyed boundary walls. Many of the squire's horses from the nearby hall were taken into the church where they survived by clinging to the pews, and it is claimed that one horse escaped by scrambling on to the altar table. Several local houses were devastated during the deluge and six people were drowned before the flood water subsided.

With its magnificent castle and delightful village setting Bamburgh draws crowds of visitors to this northerly stretch of the Northumberland coastline. Its commanding position also attracted early settlers and the castle rock became the base for local rulers. According to the Anglo-Saxon Chronicle, Ida established the kingdom of Northumbria from his camp at Bamburgh and it was his grandson, Ethelfrith the Destroyer, who passed the settlement to his wife Bebba. At this point the name was changed from Din Guardi to Bebbanburgh and it became a stronghold of the Christian faith, although most of the area remained pagan.

Items recovered from the castle precincts during excavations in 2003 indicate trade links with locations in the Arctic and mainland Europe during the Anglo-Saxon period. An intriguing discovery was a small flat piece of gold with three tiny holes for fastening to a bigger item such as a belt, scabbard or maybe even a book cover.

Bamburgh was attacked by Penda, King of Mercia, during the mid-seventh century and in the late tenth century

The interior of St Andrew's Church, Bywell.

Danish raiders caused further destruction. It is believed that Norman invaders con-structed a wooden fortress as a safe refuge for governors of Northumberland, and in 1095 the rebellious Robert Mowbray was besieged at Bamburgh by the forces of William Rufus. Rebuilt in stone during the twelfth century, Bamburgh Castle retained its strategic importance during the turbulent period of border wars. It was visited by monarchs, including King John and Henry III during the thirteenth century, and housed notable prisoners such as Piers Gaveston, favourite of Edward II, and David Bruce after the defeat of Scottish forces at Neville's Cross in 1346.

Considerable damage was inflicted by two sieges during the Wars of the Roses and there was further destruction in the mid-1640s when Royalist forces under Sir Ralph Grey were besieged by parliamentary troops led by the Earl of Northumberland.

In 1704 the castle was purchased from the Forster family by Nathaniel, Lord Crewe, Bishop of Durham, and parts of the fortress were restored to include a boarding school for thirty-four girls who were trained in domestic service. Other sectors of the castle were adapted as a free surgery and dispensary, a windmill was incorporated within the precincts and accommodation was provided for shipwrecked sailors. During the early years of the twentieth century the castle was heavily restored by the new owner, the 1st Lord Armstrong, but within the towering walls it is still possible to trace early aspects such as the enormous early Norman keep.

St Peter's Church, Bywell.

Storm conditions around Bamburgh Castle.

Bamburgh Castle viewed from the village.

During the medieval period the township of Bamburgh enjoyed considerable importance. In 1177 it contributed £18 6s 8d to the Royal Exchequer, and soon afterwards, during the thirteenth century, King Henry III granted a charter giving a number of rights to local citizens. In 1295 two representatives were sent from Bamburgh to Edward I's Model Parliament in company with members from Corbridge and Newcastle, and during the following year twenty-eight burgesses paid a special subsidy levied by the king which amount to £3 18s 10½d. This period of prosperity was halted in 1297 by Scottish raids, but during the fourteenth century the township recovered a measure of prosperity with a coastal outlet at Warenmouth providing access to the open sea. A further series of Scottish raids and destruction caused by the Wars of the Roses during the fifteenth century again reduced Bamburgh's importance, and the township was taken over by the Master of the Austin canons, who were based locally. When monasteries were closed on the orders of Henry VIII, lands passed to the Forster family whose extravagance resulted in bankruptcy. Ownership, in more recent times, has been held by Lord Crewe and Lord Armstrong.

Another indication of Bamburgh's early status is to be found within St Aidan's Church. The impressive square tower dates from the thirteenth century and other aspects of the building including the chancel were built during the same period. It was completed in about 1230 and is unusually long with a fine row of lancet arches along the upper level of the walls. Legend suggests that it covers the site of

Dorothy Forster's pear tree, Bamburgh, planted in 1663.

the Saxon church building where St Aidan died on 31 August 651. A surprising feature in Bamburgh church is the thirteenth-century vaulted crypt, which was discovered accidentally in 1837 when oak flooring was lifted from the chancel floor. It is believed to have been the home of a recluse or a repository for relics, probably associated with St Aidan.

While there are pointers to Bamburgh's earlier pre-eminence, indications of Wark-on-Tyne's importance are more difficult to identify. Located about 5 miles south of Bellingham on the upper reaches of the North Tyne, it was at one time the chief town of Tynedale. It is believed that Alfwald, King of Northumbria, was murdered here in 788 after maintaining Christian values among his citizens for the previous nine years. More than two centuries later Norman forces constructed a motte and bailey castle on the west bank of the Tyne and it became the centre for the lordship of Wark. From 1150 to the end of the thirteenth century Tynedale was part of Scotland and Scottish rulers held court here, but apart from remnants of the motte and bailey castle there is little evidence of Wark's earlier grandeur.

Wark village.

141

Index of Place-names